THE LIE THAT NAMED ME

Unwanted. Unfixable.

Unworthy.

Surviving Foster Care. Defying the Labels.

MILDRED ETHERTON

Dedication

I dedicate this book to the children who survived the foster care system, to those who endured trauma and kept going, and to the people who helped me without expecting anything in return.

I am grateful for my chosen family, and for the foster parents, guardians, staff, caseworkers, and relatives who showed kindness along the way.

If you are rebuilding your life after loss or hardship, I hope this book offers hope and reminds you of the strength you already carry.

PREFACE

The pages that follow tell the story of my life, including the violence of a brutal childhood, the instability of foster care, and the quiet strength it took to keep going when giving up would have been easier.

This is not a story written for sympathy. It is a story about survival, identity, and what it means to keep choosing life after being told, in countless ways, that you are unwanted, unfixable, or unworthy.

I wrote this book because I know my story is not unique.

There are many people who grew up in broken homes, moved through the foster care system, or learned to survive without safety, guidance, or permanence. If you are one of them, I want you to know you are not alone — and that your experiences matter, even if no one named them at the time.

This memoir is also an act of witness.

It speaks to the loneliness of displacement, the confusion of growing up without a stable identity, and the long road of learning how to live, *not just survive*, after trauma. It explores how silence shapes us, how labels can wound us, and how healing often begins long after the system moves on.

My hope is that these pages offer recognition, language, and a sense of belonging to those who have lived similar truths. I also hope they bring understanding to those who have never had to navigate these systems, and compassion for people who are often misunderstood or overlooked.

Above all, this book is a testament to resilience.

Even in the most difficult circumstances, growth is possible. Healing is not linear, and strength does not always look loud. Sometimes it looks like staying. Sometimes it looks like telling the truth for the first time.

This is my story, told honestly, without minimizing what happened or who it shaped me to be. If you are reading this, I hope you find something here that helps you feel seen.

TABLE OF CONTENTS

PART 1:
THE MAKING OF SILENCE

Silence is not the absence of sound. It is the presence of fear.

"Children don't stop speaking because they have nothing to say. They stop because no one makes it safe to be heard."

"When pain is repeated often enough, it begins to feel normal."

"Some children survive by disappearing. Others survive by becoming exactly what is expected."

"School didn't save me. But it was the first place I learned I might survive."

PART 2:
AGING OUT & LEARNING TO LIVE

PART 3:

WHAT THE SYSTEM COULDN'T GIVE ME

PART 5:

WHAT I HAD TO BUILD MYSELF

(Adulthood, survival skills, love, faith, and learning how to live without a map)

"No one teaches you how to live when survival was your first language."

"Healing doesn't only happen in therapy. Sometimes it happens in the way you stock your pantry and lock your front door."

"Safety was never something I learned by feeling it. I learned it by managing around its absence."

"Love doesn't erase trauma. It asks you to meet it honestly."

"I love my children in ways that scare me."

"Belief is not obedience when it refuses to look away."

"Family is not a title you assign. It is a relationship you earn."

"You can tell the truth without carrying it everywhere."

PART 6:

WHAT REMAINS

"We don't heal by becoming stronger. We heal by being met."

"What we needed was never perfection. It was genuine, nonjudgmental presence."

"What we needed was never perfection. It was genuine, nonjudgmental presence."

"Some people are born into comfort. Some are born into chaos. Some are born into stories they never chose. But somewhere along the way, every one of us must decide what kind of heart we will carry through the world."

The Girl I Had to Become For Myself. "She wasn't hard to love… She was just never loved the way she needed."*

PART 1

THE MAKING OF SILENCE

Chapter One

Silence is not the absence of sound. It is the presence of fear.

I learned early that quiet could keep me alive.

It wasn't something anyone taught me outright. No one sat me down and explained that words could be dangerous, that truth carried weight, or that questions could fracture what little safety existed. Silence arrived instead through observation. Through watching what happened when adults were challenged, when emotions leaked, when the wrong sentence landed in the wrong room.

In our house, noise was unpredictable. It could mean laughter, but more often it meant anger, sharp, sudden, and aimed. Raised voices carried consequences. Doors closing too hard, signaled danger. Silence, on the other hand, felt neutral. Silence did not provoke. Silence did not accuse. Silence blended into the walls, into the carpet, into the spaces where children were expected to exist without being noticed.

I became fluent in it.

My body learned before my mind ever did. I learned how to move without drawing attention, how to listen for footsteps and shifts in tone, how to read a room before entering it. I learned how to hold my breath without realizing I was doing it, how to keep my shoulders tight, my face still, my voice small. Quiet lived in my muscles long before it became a conscious choice.

Fear did not announce itself as fear back then. It disguised itself as responsibility. As awareness. As being *mature for my age*. I was praised for knowing better, for staying out of the way, for not making things harder than they already were.

There were things happening that I did not yet have language for, things that made my stomach twist and my chest feel too tight, but I understood instinctively that naming them would not make them stop. If anything, naming them might make them worse. Words felt like matches near gasoline.

So I learned not to name them.

Home was not a place of rest. It was a place of vigilance. I learned how to sit still for long periods of time, how to occupy myself quietly, how to disappear in plain sight. I learned that adults noticed children most when something was wrong, and that being noticed rarely led to protection. Attention felt conditional and dangerous, something to be avoided rather than sought.

Even my thoughts learned to stay quiet.

I became careful about what I allowed myself to feel. Fear was constant, but I treated it like background noise, something to live around rather than respond to. I did not yet know how to articulate dread or confusion or grief. I only knew how to suppress them long enough to get through the day.

At school, I was different.

School was loud, structured, predictable. Bells rang on schedule. Rules were written down. Adults followed patterns. For the first time, there were spaces where my silence was interpreted as good behavior rather than something suspicious or defiant.

Teachers praised me for being well-mannered, for being focused, for being easy.

No one asked why I never raised my hand.

No one wondered why I flinched when voices rose, or why my body stiffened when attention shifted suddenly. My quiet fit neatly into the expectations placed on good students, and so it was rewarded without question.

Silence, in those rooms, became currency.

Each compliment reinforced the same lesson I had learned at home: the less of myself I required, the safer I became. The less space I took up, the more approval I earned.

And so the lie began to form…not in words, but in identity.

That if I stayed quiet, I would be *safe*.
That if I stayed quiet, I would be *good*.
That if I stayed quiet, I *might belong*.

I carried that belief forward without questioning it, unaware that silence was not protecting me: it was shaping me.

Chapter Two

"Children don't stop speaking because they have nothing to say. They stop because no one makes it safe to be heard."

Foster care did not begin as a rescue. It began as a rupture. Nothing about it felt organized or intentional from the inside. Adults spoke in fragments, voices lowered or raised just outside the rooms where children waited. Conversations happened over my head, behind closed doors, in hallways I was told to sit quietly in. I learned quickly that information moved around me, not through me.

When the decision was made, it felt sudden, even though the conditions leading to it had been building for years. I remember being told to pack. Not being asked what I wanted to bring, just being instructed to gather my things. The word *things* felt generous. There were not many.

I stood in my room holding items that no longer felt like they belonged anywhere. Clothes that smelled like a house I was leaving. Objects that had survived chaos but could not protect me from what came next. I packed quickly into my garbage bag, afraid that hesitation might be interpreted as resistance.

No one explained where we were going.
No one explained how long we would be gone.
No one explained whether we would come back.

The absence of explanation felt deliberate, though I did not yet have the words for why. Questions had never been welcomed. Silence was safer than curiosity.

I did not cry.

Crying felt like a risk. Crying invited attention. Attention invited questions. And questions invited truths that had never led to safety before. I learned to swallow emotion before it reached my throat, to keep my face neutral, my body compliant.

The first nights in foster care were the hardest.

Every new place came with unfamiliar sounds... appliances humming, floors creaking, voices speaking softly in the next room, other children crying. I lay awake listening, mapping the house in my mind, trying to understand its rhythms before morning arrived. Sleep felt dangerous in unfamiliar spaces. Rest required trust, and trust had already been stretched thin.

I learned to keep my belongings close.

Even when I unpacked, I did so lightly, aware that permanence was an illusion. Drawers never felt like mine. Beds felt borrowed. I lived in a constant state of readiness, prepared to move again with little notice.

Foster care introduced me to a new version of silence.

This silence was institutional. It came with rules, schedules, and expectations that shifted from home to home. It came with strangers who asked questions, they did not stay long enough to hear the answers to. It came with case workers who spoke kindly but rotated frequently enough that continuity felt impossible.

Each placement required recalibration.

I learned which cupboards were off-limits, which chairs belonged to which adults, which tones of voice meant approval and which meant retreat. I learned how to be agreeable, how to minimize my presence, how to make myself easy to keep.

Agreeable children were **praised**.
Agreeable children were **easier to place**.
Agreeable children were **easier to move**.

With every transition, something in me tightened. Each move carried the same unspoken message: *you are temporary.* I was not losing homes. I was losing proof… proof that I mattered, that I was wanted, that I could be known and still chosen.

The system did not ask who I was.

It asked whether I was manageable.

So I became that.

By the time I realized how deeply this lesson had settled into me, silence was no longer something I used.

It was something I was.

Chapter Three

"When pain is repeated often enough, it begins to feel normal."

Pain did not always arrive as an emergency. Most of the time, it came quietly, routine, predictable, almost scheduled. It lived in ordinary moments, tucked inside rules and expectations framed as discipline, order, or care. Over time, my body learned to anticipate it. My muscles tightened before my mind could catch up. I learned to brace without being told.

There were no clear markers for when something crossed a line. Boundaries blurred early, and once that happened, everything that followed felt confusing rather than shocking. I did not understand that what was happening was wrong; I only understood that it was happening to me, and that reacting made it worse.

Fear became instructional.

I learned how to calculate risk with precision no child should possess. I learned which expressions invited attention and which deflected it. I learned that compliance shortened moments and resistance stretched them out. I learned to still my face, quiet my body, swallow reactions before they could surface.

Silence was no longer just protection. It was participation.

I was praised for being calm, for being cooperative, for not causing trouble. Adults mistook my withdrawal for maturity. No one questioned why a child needed so little, or why she learned so quickly to disappear.

Inside, something began to split.

There was the version of me that followed instructions, earned approval, and stayed out of the way. And there was the version of me that carried what had no safe place to go. That second version learned to stay hidden. She learned that feelings could be dangerous if witnessed, and unbearable if fully felt.

Control became my substitute for safety.

If I could not control what happened to me, I could control how I responded. I could control my grades. I could control my behavior. I could control the way my body took up space. I could control how little I needed.

I was taught, explicitly and implicitly, that nothing I did was ever quite right.

Every chore was inspected. Every homework assignment was graded again at home. The way I spoke, the way I chewed my food, the way I addressed adults, the tone of my voice, everything was monitored, corrected, critiqued. Mistakes were never neutral. They were evidence. Proof that I had failed. Proof that I deserved whatever came next.

If I did something wrong, I was punished... somehow, some way. The form varied, but the message never did.

I learned to expect correction. I learned to anticipate consequences. I learned that doing my best was irrelevant if my best still fell short.

Perfectionism did not begin as ambition. It began as armor.

Every assignment completed flawlessly felt like proof that I was worth keeping. Every rule followed precisely felt like insurance. Mistakes felt catastrophic, not only because of punishment, but because of what they seemed to confirm. Failure meant I was bad. Failure meant I needed to be fixed.

At night, when the house finally settled, my thoughts grew louder. The silence that protected me during the day turned hostile after dark. Memories replayed without permission. Sensations returned without warning. I felt trapped inside a body that remembered things my mind did not yet have language for.

That was when I learned how to hurt myself.

It did not begin as rebellion. It did not begin as a desire to die. It began as logic.

If I messed something up, I deserved to be punished. That was what I had been taught. Pain had always followed failure, so I learned to deliver it myself. Hurting my body felt like taking responsibility… like restoring order. It was the closest thing I knew to accountability.

It also brought relief.

The pain I chose felt different from the pain that arrived uninvited. It was contained. Measurable. Temporary. For a moment, it grounded me in my body instead of scattering me inside it. It gave shape to feelings that otherwise felt endless and unmanageable.

I did not want to die. I wanted the noise to stop.

Self-harm became a private language, one no adult had taught me, and one no adult noticed. I learned how to hide evidence the same way I learned to hide everything else. The secrecy did not feel deceptive. It felt necessary.

As a teenager, I stood at a bus stop while someone pulled my hair and spat in my face. I did not react. I did not tell anyone. I did not even cry. I absorbed it the way I absorbed everything else. Standing up for myself never felt like an option, it felt dangerous.

Adults praised my resilience without understanding its cost.

I was told I was strong for my age. Responsible. Independent. No one asked why independence had been required so early, or what it meant for a child to rely almost entirely on herself.

Pain became familiar enough that it stopped feeling urgent and started feeling like baseline reality. When things were calm, I felt uneasy. Chaos made sense. Calm felt temporary, suspicious.

This was how trauma trained my nervous system, not to seek safety, but to expect harm.

I learned to meet pain halfway.

I learned to anticipate disappointment before it arrived. I learned to detach before I could be abandoned. I learned to shrink emotionally so that when something was taken from me, there would be less to lose.

No one ever explained these lessons.

They were absorbed through repetition, reinforced through survival, and sealed through silence. By the time anyone noticed how well-behaved I was, how accomplished, how put together, the pattern was already embedded.

I had learned how to endure.

What I had not learned was how to be safe.

And endurance, mistaken for strength, carried me forward, well prepared to survive, and profoundly unprepared to be held.

Chapter Four

"Some children survive by disappearing. Others survive by becoming exactly what is expected."

School was the first place where my silence was mistaken for virtue.

In classrooms, quiet children were praised. We were labeled focused, respectful, mature. I learned quickly that the same behaviors that kept me safe at home made me successful at school. Sit still. Follow directions. Complete the work. Do not draw attention to yourself. These rules felt familiar, almost comforting in their predictability.

For the first time, adults smiled at me without suspicion.

Teachers spoke my name with approval. My papers came back marked with high grades and encouraging notes written neatly in the margins. Stickers appeared on assignments. Progress reports glowed. In a world where attention often preceded harm, this kind of attention felt safe. It felt earned.

No one asked why I never raised my hand.

I knew the answers. I always did. But speaking felt unnecessary, and risky. I had already learned that visibility came with consequences, and silence came with reward. So, I perfected it.

School became my refuge, not because it healed me, but because it structured me.

Schedules were posted on the wall. Bells rang when they were supposed to. Lessons began and ended on time. Adults followed patterns I could learn. That consistency soothed something inside me that was always braced for chaos. I could prepare myself for what came next.

I learned to excel quietly.

My achievements were noticed without requiring me to be seen. That distinction mattered. I could succeed without exposing myself. I could belong, without risking disruption. Silence became not just protection, but a strategy.

The lie deepened.

If adults approved of me when I disappeared, then disappearing must be good.

At home, silence had protected me. At school, it elevated me. The message was consistent across environments: my worth increased when my needs decreased.

No one noticed how tightly I gripped my pencil, or how my body stiffened when teachers raised their voices to quiet the room. No one questioned why sudden attention made my heart race, or why mistakes felt unbearable.

Those responses were misread as diligence.

Achievement became another form of armor. Grades became proof that I was functioning—that whatever had happened elsewhere had not damaged me. In truth, they were evidence of how much effort it took to appear unbroken.

I learned how to read adults the way I had learned to read danger. I knew which teachers were safe to approach and which ones preferred distance. I learned how to anticipate expectations before they were spoken. Being prepared meant staying invisible.

School also taught me something quieter—and more dangerous.

It taught me that voices mattered only when they were invited.

I learned when to speak—during roll call, when called on, and when participation was required. Outside of those narrow windows, silence was preferable. Questions slowed lessons. Emotions complicate outcomes. Stories disrupted the flow.

So, I kept mine to myself.

The parts of me shaped by fear did not disappear in these classrooms. They learned how to dress themselves in achievement. Trauma learned how to look like success.

I was never *disruptive*. Never *defiant*. Never *loud*.
I was praised for being *easy*.
But ease came at a **cost**.

Each year I spent being rewarded for silence made it harder to imagine another way of being. My voice did not vanish… it weakened. Unused. Untested. Uncertain.

By the time I sensed that something inside me wanted to speak, I no longer trusted it. I had learned that safety lived in restraint, that approval followed obedience, and that survival depended on staying within the lines others drew.

School gave me knowledge. It gave me structure. It gave me proof that I could succeed.

What it did not give me was permission.

Being quiet in the system was not a personality trait… it was a survival strategy. I learned early that silence kept me safe, or at least less visible. What I did not understand then was that being quiet also meant my needs disappeared with me.

When I was sixteen, I snapped once. I wanted to see what would happen if I acted out just one time. I walked up and hit a group home staff member in the face. I had never hit anyone before in my life. That single moment defined me more than years of compliance ever did. I was picked up from school that day and moved to another home until I apologized. Overnight, I became *the problem child.*

Other moves came without warning or wrongdoing. One home decided to take only pregnant girls. I was moved because I no longer fit the model. I overheard conversations about funding and profit, about what placements were worth. Being good had not protected me. Silence had not earned me stability. It had only made it easier to move.

And so, I carried my silence forward, polished, praised, and profoundly misunderstood, into the next chapters of my life, where being good would no longer be enough, and being quiet would begin to cost me more than it protected.

Chapter Five

"School didn't save me. But it was the first place I learned I might survive."

School was never just school to me.

It was the only place where the rules made sense. Bells rang when they were supposed to. Adults stood where they said they would. There were schedules, expectations, and beginnings and endings that didn't shift overnight. Compared to everything else in my life, that kind of predictability felt like safety.

Even when it wasn't.

I came to school carrying things no one could see. Bruises hidden under clothes. Pain I didn't yet have language for. Exhaustion that didn't come from staying up late, but from staying alert all the time. I learned early how to sit still through discomfort, how to keep my face neutral, how to pretend I was fine when I wasn't.

No one asked the right questions.

Teachers noticed I was quiet, that I followed directions, that I did my work. They praised me for being mature, responsible, resilient. I learned quickly that those words were shields. As long as I wore them well, no one looked too closely.

There were days when the pain showed up anyway.

I remember going to the nurse's office more than once, not because I believed they could fix anything, but because it was the only place I was allowed to stop. Fluorescent lights. Vinyl beds. The smell of antiseptic. I sat there waiting, hoping someone would see what I didn't know how to say.

They didn't.

Sometimes I was sent back to class with an ice pack. Sometimes with a note. Sometimes with nothing at all. The message was always the same: whatever I was carrying didn't register as urgent.

So I learned how to endure quietly.

School became a place where I could disappear into structure. I focused on assignments. On numbers. On patterns that behaved the way they were supposed to. I found comfort in subjects that had answers, in work that rewarded precision.

There was something grounding about problems that resolved if you followed the steps.

At home, there were no steps. At school, there were.

I stayed late when I could. I volunteered for things that kept me there longer. I learned how to stretch the day just enough, so I didn't have to rush back to wherever I was staying. When the final bell rang, I felt a familiar tightening in my chest.

Leaving meant uncertainty.

I watched other kids complain about school with casual confidence. They rolled their eyes, talked back, skipped assignments. They knew there would be consequences, but they also knew there would be forgiveness. They had somewhere to land.

I didn't.

I graduated a year early, not because I was ready, but because I was tired of being shuffled and I was turning eighteen. The day I finished, no one from my life was there. Instead, school counselors and administrators, people who barely knew me, threw me a small, private graduation in an office. There was a cake. A cap and gown. Kindness, I hadn't asked for.

It was sweet. And it was uncomfortable.

Being celebrated felt foreign, almost embarrassing. When I look back at yearbooks now, I'm barely there. Sometimes I wish I had slowed time down, stayed longer, learned how to belong before aging out forced me forward.

Even when they didn't understand, there were adults who saw me show up every day. Who watched me try. Who noticed my effort, even if they didn't see the cost. That mattered more than I realized at the time.

Mistakes felt dangerous. Attention felt risky. I learned how to stay just visible enough to be praised, but not visible enough to be questioned. I lived in that narrow space for years.

No one came when things were wrong.
No one intervened.
No one named what was happening.

And still, school gave me something I didn't have anywhere else: witnesses.

No one came to my school events: not to marching band, not to band concerts, not to sports. I showed up anyway.

The first time I spoke publicly, I was shaking.

I was sixteen, standing in front of people who didn't know me, holding a microphone that felt too heavy for my hands. My voice wavered. My heart raced. I could feel every eye in the room, every breath I took.

I don't remember exactly what I said. I remember how it felt to say it.

Terrifying.
Exposing.
Strangely relieving.

When the audience clapped, I felt confused. I wasn't finished. I hadn't said everything. The applause felt premature… —like they were responding to a version of me that was only partially visible.

"I'm not done yet," I said into the microphone.

The words surprised even me.

That moment didn't change my life overnight. It didn't fix anything. But it cracked something open. It was the first time I realized that speaking didn't immediately destroy me, that being heard didn't automatically lead to punishment or abandonment.

I carried that moment with me quietly.

School didn't *protect me* from abuse.
It didn't stop what was happening.
It didn't *rescue me.*

But it gave me *language.*
It gave me *structure.*
It gave me a place where my presence was at least
acknowledged.

For a long time, I believed that no one had shown up for
me. And in many ways, that was true. But I can see now that
school held me when nothing else did, not gently, not
intentionally, but consistently enough to matter.

I learned there *how to think.*
How to *articulate.*
How to stand in front of people without **disappearing**.

Those skills would come back to me later… when silence
no longer felt survivable, when carrying everything alone
became too heavy, when I realized that my story didn't
belong only to me.

School didn't give me safety. It gave me a voice.

And eventually, that voice would become the thing that
kept me from vanishing completely.

To My Teachers

School was the only place that didn't disappear on me.

Even when you didn't know what was happening at home, you gave me structure. Predictability. Expectations that made sense. You taught me that effort mattered. That my mind had value. That showing up every day counted for something.

Some of you noticed more than others. Some of you almost asked the right questions. Even when no one intervened, being seen, even partially, mattered.

You are often the first adult children like me learn to trust.

Please don't underestimate that role.

When a child is quiet, compliant, and *"easy,"* it does not always mean they are okay. Sometimes it means they are surviving. Your classroom may be the only place they can breathe without fear.

You don't have to save them.

You just have to notice them.

That can be enough to change a life.

PART 2

AGING OUT & LEARNING TO LIVE

Chapter Six

"You can leave the place that hurt you and still carry its rules inside your body."

Aging out of foster care was described to me as freedom. I was told I would finally have autonomy… choices, independence, the chance to build a life of my own. The language sounded hopeful, almost celebratory. Caseworkers spoke about adulthood as if it were a clean line I could step across, a door that would open once I turned the right age. But freedom assumes a foundation, and I was leaving without one.

There was no ceremony for the transition, no moment of acknowledgment for what had been endured or what had been lost. No one sat with me to talk about fear or grief or uncertainty. Instead, there was paperwork. Deadlines. Lists of things I was suddenly responsible for knowing how to do. The shift felt abrupt, as if childhood had been shut off mid-sentence.

I remember how quiet everything felt once the system stepped back.

For so long, my life had been measured by check-ins and appointments, caseworkers, placements, forms that followed me from one home to the next. Suddenly, that structure vanished. The absence was jarring. I had learned how to survive inside systems, not outside of them.

I did what I had always done. I adapted.

Survival had already taught me how to function without asking for help. I knew how to follow rules without understanding their purpose. I knew how to meet expectations without being told what they were. I knew how to keep moving, even when I did not know where I was going.

Independence did not feel empowering. It felt exposed.

I worried constantly about practical things… money, housing, transportation, paperwork I barely understood. I learned quickly how thin the margin for error was. There was no safety net beneath me, no one to call if I failed or fell behind. Mistakes felt dangerous. There was no room for learning slowly.

I worked harder. I needed less. I asked for nothing.

Those habits once kept me safe, and now they followed me into adulthood, unquestioned. Employers praised my reliability. Supervisors admired my work ethic. I was dependable, efficient, low maintenance. These qualities were rewarded, and that reinforcement made it harder to see the cost.

Inside, I felt hollow.

There was no pause between survival phases, no space to recalibrate. I moved directly from one form of vigilance into another. The setting changed, but the rules remained the same: do not inconvenience anyone, do not reveal weakness, do not need too much.

Loneliness settled in quietly.

Without a system watching, without adults checking boxes, there was no longer anyone measuring whether I was doing *"well."* From the outside, I appeared successful. From the inside, I felt untethered. I had responsibilities but no sense of belonging. Freedom felt isolating rather than expansive.

Relationships became complicated.

Connection required vulnerability, and vulnerability felt indistinguishable from danger. I learned how to perform closeness without fully entering it. I listened more than I spoke. I gave more than I received. I stayed useful. Usefulness felt safer than being known.

I mistook endurance for identity.

Being capable became who I was, not something I did. I was proud of how little I required, how much I could carry alone. I did not recognize this as loss. It felt like strength because it had always been rewarded.

But strength without softness begins to fracture.

My body started sending signals my mind had learned to ignore. Exhaustion settled deep into my bones. Anxiety lived just beneath my skin. Sleep came lightly and left quickly. I functioned, but I was never at rest.

Survival had followed me into adulthood.

It shaped my choices, my relationships, my sense of worth. I believed that if I stayed competent enough, quiet enough, useful enough, nothing would be taken from me. I believed that adulthood required the same restraint childhood had demanded.

I did not yet understand that adulthood would ask different questions, one's survival alone could not answer.

The identity I had built to keep me safe was beginning to crack under the weight of a life that required more than endurance.

Chapter Seven

"When survival becomes your personality, you lose sight of who you were before the damage began."

Adulthood did not arrive with clarity. It arrived with expectations I knew how to meet and questions I did not know how to answer.

People asked who I was, what I liked, what I wanted, and where I saw myself going. These questions were meant to be casual, even hopeful, but they landed heavily. I had learned how to function, not how to define myself. Survival had taught me what to avoid, not what to choose.

I built relationships the same way I had built safety as a child: carefully, strategically, without revealing too much. I knew how to be attentive, supportive, present. I listened well. I noticed details. I anticipated needs before they were spoken. These qualities made me easy to be around… dependable, trustworthy.

They also kept me hidden.

Being needed felt familiar. Being wanted felt uncertain.

I gravitated toward roles where competence was valued and emotional distance was normalized. Work offered structure. Responsibility offered identity. Achievement offered proof that I was still doing something right. I poured myself into tasks and timelines, believing productivity could quiet the restlessness that followed me everywhere.

It never did.

Inside, I carried a persistent sense that something was missing, though I could not name what it was. I had learned to distrust my own needs so thoroughly that when they surfaced, they felt foreign, almost intrusive. I dismissed them quickly. Needing felt dangerous. Depending felt irresponsible.

Relationships reflected this imbalance.

I gave more than I received and told myself that was generosity. I tolerated distance and called it independence. I stayed quiet about discomfort and called it maturity. In truth, I was repeating patterns I had never had the chance to unlearn.

Conflict terrified me.

Not because I feared disagreement, but because I feared abandonment. Any sign of tension triggered the same internal alarms I had learned as a child. My body reacted before my mind could reason. My chest tightened. My thoughts scattered. I apologized instinctively, even when I was not at fault. I learned how to make myself smaller in moments that required steadiness.

I believed that if I could just be good enough, calm enough, accommodating enough, I would be safe. But adulthood does not reward disappearance the way childhood sometimes does.

Over time, the strain of maintaining this version of myself became harder to ignore. Exhaustion was no longer something I could push through quietly. Anxiety seeped into my thoughts, my sleep, my body. I felt disconnected from my own life… present, but not fully participating.

I had built a life that looked stable from the outside. Inside, I felt unanchored.

There was grief beneath that feeling, a grief I did not yet understand. Grief for a self that had never been allowed to form. Grief for choices I did not know how to make because I had never been taught that I was allowed to want anything at all.

Survival had given me tools, but it had also taken options.

It shaped my instincts, my relationships, my sense of worth. It had taught me how to endure discomfort indefinitely while convincing me that asking for more was unreasonable.

I did not yet have language for trauma. I did not know how to trace these patterns back to their origins. I only knew that something inside me was tired of living on alert.

The identity I had built, capable, dependable, low-need, was beginning to feel like a cage.

And for the first time, I sensed that continuing this way might cost me more than changing ever had.

That realization marked the beginning of a quiet shift, one that would eventually force me to confront the truths I had learned to avoid, and the story I had been telling myself about who I was allowed to be.

Chapter Eight

"There comes a moment when the strategies that once kept you alive begin to ask for more than they can give."

The unraveling did not happen all at once. It came quietly, disguised as normal life… missed sleep, constant tension, a body that refused to relax even when nothing was wrong. I told myself this was ordinary exhaustion. Adulthood was demanding. Everyone was tired. Everyone felt overwhelmed sometimes.

But my tiredness felt different.

It was not the fatigue of effort alone. It was the exhaustion of vigilance, the kind that settles deep into the nervous system and never fully leaves. Even in moments of calm, my body stayed alert, waiting for the next shift in tone, the next disappointment, the next thing I would need to absorb without reaction.

Survival was no longer just a response. It was reflex.

I began to notice how quickly I apologized, how instinctively I took responsibility for discomfort that did not belong to me. I apologized for taking up space. I apologized for having needs. I apologized for emotions I had not yet expressed. My body reacted before my mind had time to decide whether an apology was warranted.

I noticed how difficult it was to say no.

Even small refusals felt dangerous. Declining invitations, setting boundaries, expressing disagreement... all of it triggered the same internal alarms I had learned as a child. My chest tightened. My thoughts scattered. I felt the familiar urge to make things smooth again, to restore balance by shrinking myself.

The cost of being low-need was becoming visible.

In my relationships, I gave steadiness, patience, and understanding. I absorbed discomfort quietly. I listened more than I spoke. I adjusted constantly. I rarely asked for the same care in return. When my needs surfaced, they arrived tentatively... muted, uncertain, easy to dismiss.

I learned how to talk myself out of wanting before anyone else had the chance to hear it.

Faith entered my life quietly. Not as certainty. Not as answers. But as a question that would not let go.

I was drawn to the idea that worth might exist independent of performance, that love might not need to be earned through usefulness or restraint. These ideas felt almost impossible to trust. If they were true, then everything I had built myself around was incomplete.

Faith invited stillness. Trauma resisted it.

Stillness left room for memories. It left room for grief. It left room for questions I had survived by avoiding. I wanted the comfort faith promised without the vulnerability it required. I wanted reassurance without surrender.

My body began to push back.

Anxiety no longer stayed contained beneath the surface. It leaked into my thoughts, my sleep, my ability to focus. Panic arrived without warning, untethered from immediate threats. I felt unsafe in situations that were objectively stable.

This confused me.

I had done everything right. I had followed the rules. I had worked hard, stayed quiet, avoided trouble. I had built a life that looked secure. The equation no longer made sense.

The truth, slowly, became harder to ignore. Survival had reached its limit.

The tools that had protected me as a child were no longer sufficient for the life I was living. What had once minimized harm was now magnifying it. Avoidance was isolating. Silence was suffocating. Control was exhausting.

I began to sense that something inside me was asking for more than endurance.

Not loudly.
Not dramatically.
Just persistently.

It showed up as restlessness. As sadness without a clear source. As a longing I could not explain. I felt grief for something unnamed. A life I had not lived because I had been too busy surviving the one I was given.

That realization frightened me.

If survival were no longer enough, then I would have to risk change. And change had always felt more dangerous than staying the same.

Still, the cracks widened.

I could not unknow what I was beginning to feel. I could not return to the certainty that silence alone would keep me safe. The identity I had worn so carefully, *capable, dependable, low-need*, was starting to collapse under its own weight.

I stood at the edge of a reckoning I did not yet understand.

All I knew was this: continuing as I was, would cost me more than I could afford, and something deeper was asking - *quietly, insistently* -to be heard for the first time.

The voice I had trained to wait, was no longer willing to stay silent.

Chapter Nine

"The truth does not arrive all at once. It comes in pieces, and it asks if you are willing to hold them."

I had spent most of my life avoiding questions that did not come with clear answers. Questions required honesty, and honesty carried risk. For years, avoidance had worked. It kept me functional, composed, intact enough to move forward. But once the cracks appeared, avoidance lost its authority.

The unease that had followed me for years was no longer content to stay unnamed.

I began to notice how instinctively I minimized my own experiences when I spoke about my past. I softened language without realizing I was doing it. I replaced specifics with generalities. I framed harm as misunderstanding, pain as inconvenience. These habits felt automatic, like breathing. They were not about deception—they were about survival.

But survival was no longer enough.

Therapy entered my life quietly, without ceremony or conviction. I did not arrive hopeful. I arrived cautious, prepared to manage impressions the same way I always had.

I told myself I was there for practical reasons, stress, anxiety, exhaustion. Those explanations felt acceptable. They did not require me to confront the deeper truth: that something inside me had been fractured for a long time.

Sitting across from someone whose role was simply to listen felt deeply unsettling.

There was no performance to hide behind. No task to complete. No version of myself could earn approval through competence. Silence, which had once protected me, functioned differently in that room. It invited questions. Gentle ones. Patient ones. The kind that waited longer than I was comfortable with.

I learned quickly how skilled I was at deflection.

I spoke about events without emotion. I narrated experiences as if they had happened to someone else. I analyzed patterns instead of feeling them. I used insight to avoid vulnerability. These strategies had served me well for years, and part of me resented the way they were no longer enough.

The therapist noticed.

She did not interrupt or correct me. She did not push. She waited. That patience unsettled me more than confrontation would have. I had learned how to navigate anger, disappointment, and authority. I did not know how to navigate presence without demand.

Over time, patterns began to surface.

The perfectionism. The self-erasure. The way my body reacted to raised voices or sudden changes. The way my chest tightened before my thoughts could catch up. These were not personality quirks or individual failures. They were responses… learned, repeated, reinforced.

Naming that truth destabilized me.

If these patterns had been shaped by harm, then the harm itself had been real. And if it had been real, my silence would not of been maturity or strength. It had been survival.

That realization carried grief.

Grief for the child who had adapted so well that no one noticed how much adaptation had cost. Grief for the version of myself that might have existed if safety had not been conditional. Grief for the years I spent believing that needing less made me more worthy.

I felt anger, too.

Anger at systems that rewarded compliance instead of protection. Anger at adults who mistook silence for resilience. Anger at how easily a child's identity could be shaped by environments that demanded endurance instead of care.

Truth complicated my faith.

I had been drawn to the idea of unconditional love, but now I was forced to confront how unfamiliar it felt. If love did not require performance, then I would have to learn how to receive it without earning it first. That felt terrifying. Faith invited surrender and surrender required trust, something I had learned to ration carefully.

As more pieces came into view, my past began to reorganize itself.

Moments I had dismissed as insignificant took on new meaning. Reactions I had blamed on weakness revealed their logic. Nothing about me was broken. I had been responding exactly as someone in my position would.

That understanding brought **relief**, and **responsibility**.

Relief, because it softened the shame I had carried for years. Responsibility, because once something is named, it cannot be ignored. Awareness demanded change and change required risk.

I was not healed.

I was not suddenly brave or free. Therapy did not erase the past or quiet my nervous system overnight. But something had shifted. The story I told myself about who I was *capable, independent, unaffected* no longer held.

The silence that had once protected me was losing its authority.

And for the first time, I began to consider what it might mean to live not just in survival, but in truth… even if that truth required me to feel things I had spent a lifetime avoiding.

PART 3

WHAT THE SYSTEM COULDN'T GIVE ME

Chapter Ten

"We don't age out of trauma. We age into understanding it."

I did not write this letter in a moment of anger. I wrote it in a moment of clarity.

By the time I reached the age when support quietly disappeared, I had already learned that survival does not follow neat timelines. I had watched doors close with bureaucratic finality *funding ends, programs expire, eligibility shifts* as if the hardest part of my life had already passed.

It hadn't.

At eighteen, I was not planning a future. I was trying to stay alive. I was learning how to feed myself consistently, how to sleep without fear, how to exist in a world without constant supervision or a safety net beneath me. Independence was not empowering; it was overwhelming.

At twenty-one, I was still learning who I was.

Identity does not emerge on command, especially when childhood has been spent adapting to chaos. At twenty-one, I was not behind. I was delayed by design. I was assembling the most basic pieces of myself without context, guidance, or permission to move slowly.

By twenty-five, when the system decided I should be finished needing support, I was only beginning to understand what had happened to me.

That understanding did not arrive suddenly. It came through exhaustion. Through therapy. Through the quiet realization that surviving trauma requires more than grit. It requires time. It requires safety. It requires access to support long after the crisis phase ends.

That is when I wrote this letter.

To the People Who Design and Defend the System

I need you to listen without becoming defensive.

Why do foster youth lose access to education funds at twenty-five, as if trauma follows a schedule? As if healing is linear. As if survival leaves room for long-term planning.

At eighteen, I was trying to stay alive.
At twenty-one, I was still learning who I was.

At twenty-five, I was only beginning to understand what had happened to me.
We do not age out of trauma.
We age into understanding it.

Trauma affects the brain. It alters decision-making, memory, emotional regulation, and the ability to imagine a future. Expecting children raised in chaos to know what they want to do with the rest of their lives by a certain age ignores everything we know about development. Silence, compliance, and appearing *"well-adjusted"* are often mistaken for readiness when they are actually signs of survival.

Extend the timelines. Fund the long road. Treat education as repair, not reward. Stop measuring success by speed and start measuring it by sustainability.

If the system truly exists to protect children, then it must also protect their futures... not just until it becomes inconvenient.

I did not write these words as theory.
I wrote them from lived experience.

Education was the only thing consistently out of reach for me. Not because I did not want it. Not because I did not value it. But because survival came first.

When I left the system, there was no opportunity to save. I worked because I had to eat. I paid bills because there was no one else to pay them. There was no margin for long-term planning, no one explaining how today's decisions would echo decades later. I was surviving adulthood in real time ... without guidance, without counseling, without anyone teaching me the rules I was expected to follow.

I did not understand student loans.
I did not understand interest.
I did not understand how debt could follow someone for life.

All I understood was this: I needed a diploma if I wanted a chance at stability. That message had been repeated so often it felt like truth.

But when I finally reached a place where I could pursue education intentionally – when I finally understood myself well enough to choose a path – the support that once existed was gone. The timelines had closed. The funds had expired. The grace that should accompany delayed development had disappeared.

Instead of support, I inherited debt.

Like many people who endure prolonged trauma, I entered a helping field. Survivors are often drawn to care, to service, to work that makes suffering mean something. These professions are not chosen for wealth. They are chosen because pain sharpens empathy.

But empathy does not replace financial stability.
Purpose does not absorb interest.
Compassion does not undo structural disadvantage.

I live rural, not because it was my dream, but because it was what I could afford. Access to higher-paying careers often requires relocation, flexibility, and financial risk... things that are impossible when adulthood begins already burdened by debt and responsibility. I wanted a family, so I created one. I built what I never had.

That choice mattered to me.

It still does.
But it made everything harder.

I am years into adulthood and still do not own a home. I do not have equity. I do not have inherited stability. What I have is responsibility... carried carefully, constantly, without a margin for error.

Education does not replace parents.
It does not replace guidance.
It does not replace the ability to fail safely.

For many of us, adulthood begins without a safety net. We appear functional. We work. We contribute. And still, there is no one who knew us as children, no one who can say, *I remember who you were before all of this.*

That absence does not show up on outcome reports. But it shapes everything.

I was twenty-nine when I finally began seeking therapy. When I finally had the language, the safety, and the capacity to face what had happened to me. Therapy did not arrive early. It arrived when survival loosened its grip just enough to make space for healing.

By then, the system had already decided I was finished.

The system measures success by speed: how quickly someone enrolls, graduates, and becomes *"independent."* Sustainability tells a different story. Sustainability asks whether someone can build a life without carrying permanent consequences for surviving first.

I did not age out of need.
I aged into understanding.

And it was only then – when I truly understood what education and healing were meant to be – that the system had already decided I no longer deserved help.

To the CASA Volunteers Who Showed Up

There were people in the system who did not treat me like paperwork.

I do not remember all of your names. But I remember how you made me feel.

I remember the CASA who gave me my first teddy bear... soft, ordinary, and life-changing. I took it home with me, and every time I held it, it reminded me that someone had cared without being required to. That compassion stayed with me long after the visit ended.

I remember the older couple, husband and wife, who took me to buy a dress for my eighth-grade graduation. No one had ever shown that much interest in one of my milestones before. You showed up. You stayed present. You made space for something that mattered to me.

You took me out for food and did not rush me. You sat across from me, looked me in the eyes, and listened... not to assess, not to fix, but to understand. For the first time, attention did not feel transactional. It felt human.

What set you apart was not authority.
It was a connection.

You did not treat my life like a case file. You treated it like a story worth sitting with. That mattered more than you may ever know.

Even when I returned to placements that felt cold or temporary, that teddy bear stayed with me. It became proof that care could exist without conditions. That kindness did not always come with an agenda.

You showed me that something different was possible. **And that mattered.**

Chapter Eleven

"You cannot heal what you don't yet have language for."

For most of my life, support was defined narrowly. There were case workers. There were programs. There were services attached to eligibility and age. On paper, I was supported. In practice, I was surviving alone. What existed around me was not the same as what reached me.

I was insured.

That fact is often cited as evidence that help was available. But insurance does not teach you how to ask for help. It does not explain what therapy is for. It does not tell a traumatized young adult that needing support is not failure.

For years, I believed that functioning meant healing.

If I was working, paying bills, and staying out of crisis, then I must be okay. I did not understand that survival could masquerade as wellness, or that trauma could live quietly beneath productivity. No one had ever explained that the absence of visible collapse did not mean the absence of harm.

At eighteen, I was not ready for therapy.

Not because I did not need it, but because I did not yet know what had happened to me. I was still inside the habits that had kept me alive: silence, compliance, endurance. Therapy requires awareness, and awareness takes time to develop when your nervous system has been shaped by instability.

At twenty-one, I was still learning who I was.

Identity came before healing. I needed language before I could process experience. I needed safety before I could examine memory. But the system assumes readiness based on age, not development. Support was offered early, briefly, and conditionally, then removed before it could be used.

By my late twenties, something shifted.

I began to notice patterns I could no longer ignore. The anxiety that never fully rested. The exhaustion that sleep did not fix. The way my body reacted to conflict long before my mind could respond. I was no longer just tired… I was aware.

That awareness did not arrive because support had been consistent. It arrived because survival had finally slowed enough for truth to surface.

That is when I realized I needed therapy.

Not as crisis management. Not as correction. But as understanding. As translation. As a way to finally make sense of a life that had been lived in reaction for so long.

But by then, access looked different.

Support systems were fragmented. Time was limited. Providers were scarce. Especially where I lived. Rural access meant fewer options, longer waits, less continuity. Help existed in theory, but reaching it required time, money, transportation, and emotional energy… all things already stretched thin.

No one had ever taught me how to seek support.

There had been no adult to model what it looked like to ask for help without consequences. No one had explained that therapy was not an admission of weakness, or that counseling could be preventative rather than corrective. I was learning these things alone, years later, while carrying responsibilities that left little room for collapse.

The system treats support as an intervention. But for people who grow up without families, support must be a foundation.

Therapy does not undo the absence of parents. Counseling does not replace guidance. But without them, adulthood becomes a series of self-taught lessons learned under pressure, without margin for error.

By the time I understood that I needed help, I was already expected to be done needing it.

This is not a failure of effort. It is a failure of timing.

Healing does not begin when services are offered. It begins when a person is ready to understand what they lived through.

For many of us, that readiness arrives years after the system has moved on.

And when support is delayed, its absence echoes forward, shaping relationships, decision-making, and the quiet loneliness of carrying everything alone.

Chapter Twelve

"The children who screamed were punished. The children who disappeared were praised. Both were hurting."

When I was a child, I believed misbehavior was a kind of sentence.

The kids who acted out were watched more closely. They were spoken about in lowered voices. They were pulled aside, written up, corrected, restrained. Their pain was visible. Loud enough to disrupt rooms and routines. Because of that, it was named, even if it was misunderstood.

They were labeled *bad*.
Difficult.
Behaviorally challenging.

I learned early that this kind of attention came at a cost.

It wasn't always gentle. It wasn't always protective. But it was attention. And I understood, instinctively, that attention was dangerous. I watched what happened to kids who couldn't keep their pain contained, and I decided, without ever saying it out loud, —that I would not be one of them.

So I became good. Being good was not a personality trait. It was a survival strategy.

I learned that grades mattered. Performance mattered. Compliance mattered. I learned that doing everything right kept me out of sight and out of reach. At home, perfection was demanded. Anything less invited punishment—sometimes severe, sometimes unpredictable, always instructive.

I did not perform because I wanted praise. I performed because I wanted safety.

School reinforced this lesson. Good grades were rewarded. Quiet behavior was praised. I was described as mature, responsible, and resilient. No one asked why I was so controlled, or why my body seemed perpetually braced. No one questioned what it cost a child to be that careful all the time.

I watched other kids be described as problems.

They needed more services. More supervision. More intervention. Their files were thicker. Their names came up more often in meetings. Their struggles were documented, discussed, pathologized.

Mine were not.

Looking back, I understand something I could not see then: Pain does not always present as disruption. Sometimes it presents as perfection.

Sometimes it presents as a child who never asks for help, never causes trouble, never needs anything. Sometimes it presents as compliance so complete that it becomes invisible.

I was never flagged as concerning. And that absence of concern was treated as success.

No one asked why I was excelling under conditions that should have broken me. No one asked why my silence was so absolute, or why my performance was so relentless. No one considered that a child who never falters might be hiding something far more dangerous than defiance.

Later, as an adult, I read my court documents.

I read words that had been written about me by people who had never known me beyond reports and observations. In one of those documents, a judge described me as damaged.

That word landed with more force than anything else I read.

Damaged.

It suggested something broken beyond repair. Something defective. Something fundamentally flawed.

I am not damaged. What I was, what we were, was **conditioned**.

> Conditioned to *perform*.
> Conditioned to *comply*.
> Conditioned to *survive*.

The system knows how to respond to disruption. It does not know how to respond to disappearance. Children who act out are seen as problems to be managed. Children who act in are treated as evidence that things are working.

Both interpretations are wrong.

> *Behavior is* communication.
> *Silence* is communication.
> *Perfection* is communication.

But the system only listens when the message is loud.

By rewarding compliance and punishing disruption, we teach children in care that safety depends on how well they hide their pain. We teach them that being **"good"** is safer than being honest, and that meeting expectations matters more than being seen.

Years later, the cost of that lesson becomes clear.

The *"bad"* kids carry records that follow them.
The *"good"* kids carry wounds no one ever
documented.
Neither was damaged.

We were responding exactly as children do when survival is required, and safety is conditional.

If the system wants to protect children, it must learn to see beyond behavior. It must learn to question perfection as much as defiance, and to understand that the absence of problems is not the absence of harm.

I was not damaged.

I was doing exactly what I had been taught to do.

84

Chapter Thirteen

"Loneliness is not being alone. It is having no one to return to."

There are certain days that expose loneliness more than others.

Birthdays are one of them.

Even now, birthdays hurt in a way I struggle to explain to people who have always had families. The day arrives, and with it comes a quiet reckoning, not because I expect celebration, but because birthdays are meant to be witnessed. They are meant to mark your existence in the eyes of people who have known you across time.

For me, birthdays have always been quiet.

There is no one who remembers my first one. No one tells stories about who I was as a child. No one who says, *I've watched you grow.* Each year feels less like a celebration and more like a private acknowledgment of survival.

That ache never fully went away. It changed when I became a parent.

For my children, birthdays are sacred. I make sure they are celebrated loudly and warmly… cake, decorations, traditions, people gathered together. I do this not because it comes naturally, but because I know what it feels like to grow up without it. I want my children to assume they matter enough to be celebrated.

In giving that to them, I feel both joy and grief.

Joy, because I am breaking a cycle.
Grief, because no one ever did this for me.

Holidays carry a different kind of loneliness.

They are louder and more public. Grocery stores fill with families shopping together. Churches fill with parents and children sitting shoulder to shoulder, generations sharing space. Casual conversations become reminders, *What are you doing for the holidays? Are you traveling to see family?*

I learn to answer lightly.

What I don't say is that holidays feel like standing on the outside of something everyone else seems to know how to enter. There is no home to return to, no parents to call, no table that is automatically mine. Rituals others inherit feel inaccessible, like a language I was never taught.

Walking into church during certain seasons is especially hard.

I believe in faith, but faith does not erase longing. Sitting among families, watching children lean into parents, watching people leave together, reminds me of what was meant to be. Community. Belonging. Continuity.

Sometimes, the longing turns into something harder to admit. Sometimes I wish I had a mother and father to go to.

Not to *fix* anything.
Not to *help* financially.

Just to listen. To say my name. To ask how I'm doing and mean it. And sometimes the thought goes even further than that.

Sometimes I wish I had stayed, even inside the abuse, because at least then I would have had my family.

That truth is uncomfortable. It feels wrong to say out loud. But it is honest. Abuse leaves scars, but abandonment leaves absence. There is a particular grief that comes from losing not just people, but the idea of ever having people at all.

Loneliness has shaped my adulthood quietly and constantly.

There is no one to call when I don't know if I'm doing things right, especially as a parent. No one to reassure me that I'm enough. No one whose voice carries shared history. I parent without role models, without inherited wisdom, without a safety net.

I second-guess myself more than I admit.

Am I doing this right?
Am I giving my children what they need—or just what I never had?
Am I enough?

There is no one to ask. Success feels different when there is no one to share it with.

There is no parent to make proud. No family to celebrate milestones. Achievements land quietly, acknowledged internally, then folded back into responsibility. Joy becomes private. Pride becomes restrained.

No one is there to *cry with me* when things fall apart.
No one is there to *hold me* when I am tired.
No one is there to *lift me up* or *remind me* who I am when I forget.

This loneliness does not end when the system does. It expands.

It follows you into adulthood, into parenting, into faith, into ordinary moments—standing in line at a store, sitting in a church pew, watching families move through the world together.

Sometimes, it turns inward.

Journal Entry

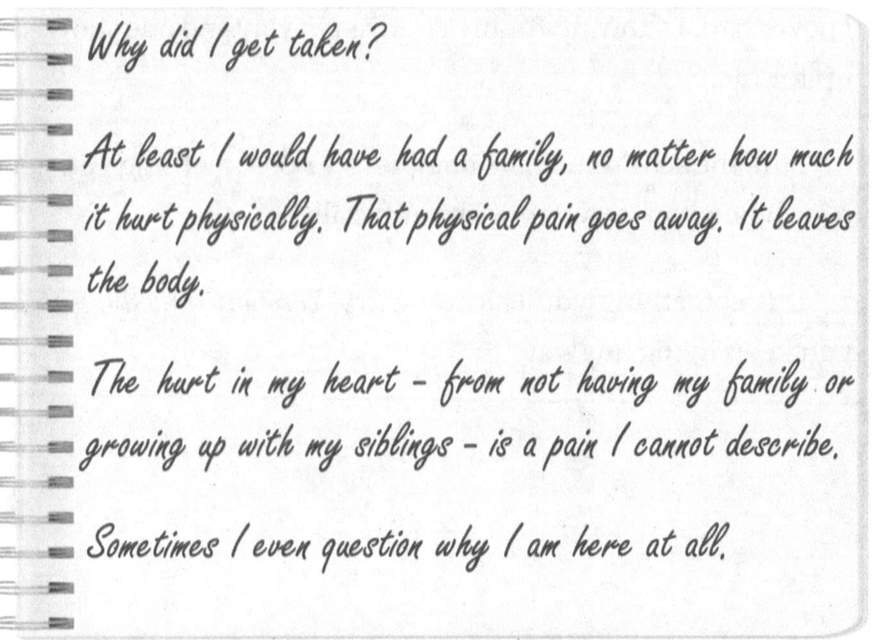

These are not thoughts born of weakness.

They are questions shaped by absence. Questions that surface when there is no one to reflect your worth back to you, no one to remind you that you belong simply because you exist. When survival becomes routine, and connection remains elusive, the mind looks for explanations.

Why me?
Why this life?
Why the silence where family should be?

I carry these questions with me, not because they define me, but because they reveal what was missing. I built the life I never had. I show up for my children in ways no one showed up for me.

Still, the ache remains. Loneliness is not something you get over when you grow up without family.

It is something you learn to carry, *carefully, quietly,* while you keep living anyway.

PART 4

THE TRUTH THAT CAME TOO LATE

(Family, identity, grief, and what silence stole)

Chapter Fourteen

"Some truths don't arrive to heal you. They arrive to explain you."

I did not grow up knowing my mother.
I grew up with a version of her.

She was spoken about in fragments and diagnoses. Mentally ill. Unstable. Unfit. The language was clinical and dismissive, as if it explained everything that had happened and excused everything that followed. She was framed as the reason we were taken, the reason we were lost, the reason our family fractured.

I accepted that story because it was the only one I was given.

For most of my life, my mother existed as an absence filled in by other people's words. I built an image of her without ever seeing her clearly... someone dangerous, incapable, someone I needed to be protected from. I carried that belief quietly, never questioning who it served.

It wasn't until much later that I learned how incomplete that picture was.

When I finally met her as an adult, I was unprepared for what I saw.

She was not the monster I had imagined. She looked nothing like the single picture I had known of her my whole life. Worn. Fragile in ways I did not yet have language for. I felt something shift immediately. Not fear, but responsibility. A pull I didn't understand, as if the roles had reversed and it was now my job to care for her.

She died young.
Fifty years old.
And with her death came silence… followed by paper.

Sorting through her belongings felt like trespassing into a life I had never been allowed to know. Documents. Articles. Notes written in handwriting I recognized only by blood. That is when I found the letter.

It was written on the back of an article titled *Bottle Babies*.

I did not know what to expect when I turned the page. What I found was my mother, *not as a diagnosis, not as a cautionary tale*, but as a woman trying to make sense of what she had survived and what she had been forced to witness with her own children.

Reading it felt like hearing her voice for the first time.

My mother's letter
(found after her death, written in cursive)

Although I have accepted the fact that my parents were alcoholics and that the way I grew up wasn't really the best, well, I'll call it a tragedy if I may, because now I'm thirty years old and I still have nightmares.

I wake up to realize these nightmares are real. I actually lived them. This is where the pain comes, and along with the pain, the questions. And no matter what, there is never a good enough answer as I try to put all the past to rest.

The harder I try, the more I hurt over and over again. I ask, why me, yet I know I'm not the only one in this world.

I become restless and impatient, mostly uncomfortable with my past. It haunts me even when I think everything is okay. It's somewhere tugging at me.

I can sit and look at the girls, and I see so much of me in their eyes. It scares me to react too quickly. Although I really don't believe I could ever hurt my kids the way I was hurt.

There are so many pieces of the puzzle missing. I would be scared to death to remember all of the past, but now that I do remember what I do, — through dreams or just looking at my kids doing something familiar, — somehow I start to feel a lot of uncertainty.

I ask myself how much I have to take. I lived my past once. Must I continue to live it and be in that fear the rest of my life?

Somehow, it doesn't seem fair.

I sat with that letter for a long time.

What struck me was not just what she said, but how familiar it felt. The questions. The restlessness. The fear of repeating harm. The sense that the past never truly stays in the past. I recognized myself in her words in a way that unsettled me.

No one had ever told me this about her.

No one had told me she tried to protect me. She brought me to the hospital. She tried to explain what was happening inside her home. She tried to speak, and was dismissed.

I learned, slowly and painfully, that my mother had not been silent. She had not been believed.

There were other truths buried in the paperwork.

The man I had been told was my father was not my biological father. He knew it. He signed my birth certificate anyway. The lie followed me my entire life, shaping my identity without my consent.

I was the affair baby. That truth did not surface until I was thirty-five years old. By then, the damage of not knowing had already been done.

Learning who my real father was, and confronting him while he was incarcerated, became its own reckoning. One that forced me to revisit everything I thought I knew about where I came from and why I was here.

But this letter was the beginning.

It was the first time I saw my mother not as a failure, but as a survivor. Not as someone who abandoned me, but as someone who was drowning without support, much like I had been.

I never knew her story while she was alive. By the time I met her, around twenty years old, she had been medicated for years and was no longer able to speak fully for herself. It was heartbreaking to witness how her depression and diagnoses overtook her life.

I only found her truth after she was gone.

And with that realization came a grief that felt almost unbearable, not only for the mother I lost, but for the truth that arrived too late to change anything between us.

Chapter Fifteen

"The deepest betrayal isn't being lied to—it's being told your pain isn't real."

For most of my life, I lived under a name that was never mine.

I believed I was one of five children, bound by a shared father, a shared last name, a shared origin story. His name was on my birth certificate. His name became my identity. And yet, even as a child, I felt like an outsider, as if I were standing behind glass, watching a family I belonged to only on paper.

I didn't look like them.

My skin tone was different. My hair and eyes didn't match. I had hearing loss. I loved music and school in ways that felt foreign to the household. My siblings fit together seamlessly. I did not. I learned early not to ask why.

Still, I held tight to what I had been told.

Identity, when you grow up without safety, becomes something you cling to, even when it hurts. I carried the belief that he was my father like fragile glass, careful not to examine the cracks too closely.

But the truth has a way of leaking through.

I remember being eight or nine years old, watching him drunkenly fall from a ladder. His head slammed into the ground. I ran to him in terror, kneeling beside his body, afraid he might die. He looked up at me and said, almost casually, *"I'm not your real dad. I just showed up to sign the papers."*

I told myself it was nothing.

I told myself it was alcohol talking. I brushed it aside because the alternative was unbearable. Children will accept almost any explanation if it allows them to keep the world intact.

What I didn't know then was that he wasn't confused. He knew.

He knew he was not my biological father, and he signed my birth certificate anyway. He claimed me in ink while denying me in action. He took my name, and then used his power over me to hurt me.

The man who named me was my abuser.

That truth would not fully surface until decades later, but it shaped everything long before I had words for it.

The abuse made more sense after.

The way I was treated differently. The way love was withheld. The way violence found me more easily. Maybe he knew I wasn't his. Maybe that knowledge hardened something in him. Maybe I became a reminder of a betrayal he could not forgive.

I will never forget telling a therapist I saw as a teenager about that memory, about him saying he wasn't my father. She told me I was deflecting. She said my feelings of not belonging were denial, projection, imagination.

I believed her.

I learned to doubt myself before anyone else could. But knowing doesn't always heal. Sometimes it shatters.

In 2016, after the birth of my son, a miracle after years of infertility, the truth arrived without warning. A message appeared on my phone from a man claiming to be my father's biological brother, asking if I would consider a DNA test.

I told myself it meant nothing.

Why would I want anything to do with that family? Why open wounds that had already scarred over? But curiosity has a way of unearthing what silence tries to bury.

A few years later, I received the results of the DNA testing I had done almost casually. At the time, I expected nothing to come from it. I wasn't searching for family. I was searching for confirmation. Proof that what I remembered was real. Proof that I had not imagined abuse to survive it.

I had not. I was thirty-five years old.

Thirty-five, and everything I thought I knew collapsed. I didn't sleep for months. My mind spiraled through rage, grief, and suspicion. The abuse. The exclusion. The distance. All of it began to make sense in ways that felt both validating and devastating.

When I followed the trail, hoping for clarity, I landed in the wrong place entirely. On paper, I matched with men old enough to be my father. For a moment, I let myself hope.

That hope did not last. It wasn't them. It was their father.

Through additional paternity testing, a man old enough to be my grandfather was confirmed as my biological father. Another blow. Another fracture. Another reminder that even truth can wound when it arrives too late or in the wrong form.

The deepest betrayal wasn't the lie. It was the years spent being told my pain wasn't real.

At nineteen, I asked my birth mother directly if the man who signed my birth certificate was my father. She looked me in the eye and said yes. Another adult choosing secrecy over truth. Protection of the system over protection of the child.

When I finally learned the truth about my biological father, I also learned I would never meet him. He was already gone.

There would be no confrontation. No answers. No chance to ask why or who he was. Only fragments… siblings, stories, and a single photograph of me as a baby. The first time I saw myself held in my mother's arms. I stared at it like I was seeing myself for the first time.

I sobbed. Because by then, the man who should have named me was dead too.

No reckoning. No accountability. Just paper trails, fabricated origin stories, and silence.

I look at my birth certificate now and see his name.

The *man* who hurt me.
The *man* who kept me from my truth.

The *man* whose name still follows me… on documents, on records, on my children's paperwork.

I cannot scrub him from the ink. He claimed me, knowing the truth. And that *lie* became the foundation of my life.

Chapter Sixteen

"They called it denial, but I knew the truth. And knowing didn't heal me. It shattered me."

The truth did not arrive gently.

It came through data. Through percentages and matches and names on a screen. It came without ceremony, without anyone sitting beside me to explain what it meant. There was no warning for how completely it would undo me.

I was thirty-five years old.

Thirty-five, with a life already built... children, responsibilities, a history I thought I understood. And in a single moment, that history collapsed. The DNA results didn't just tell me who my father wasn't. They told me who I had never been allowed to be.

For years, I had carried a quiet knowing in my body. A sense of not belonging that never fully went away. I had tried to name it before. I had tried to explain it in therapy, in conversations, in memories that didn't quite line up. Each time, I was told I was projecting. That trauma was distorting my perception.

They called it **denial**. But denial doesn't feel like this.

Denial *avoids*.
Denial *numbs*.
Denial *protects*.

What I felt was certainty without proof, and that certainty was dismissed.

When the proof finally came, it didn't soothe me. It didn't validate me in the way people imagine truth will. It detonated everything I had worked so hard to stabilize. I stopped sleeping. My thoughts raced in relentless loops, replaying childhood moments with new clarity and unbearable meaning.

The *abuse* made sense.
The *exclusion* made sense.
The *silence* made sense.

That clarity was devastating. The man who abused me had known I wasn't his. He signed my birth certificate anyway.

That fact lodged itself in my chest like a weight I couldn't dislodge. It reframed every interaction, every punishment, every moment of cruelty. I wondered how long he had known. I wondered if my existence itself had been a reminder of a betrayal he resented, and whether that resentment had shaped the violence I endured.

Knowing this didn't bring **closure**.

It brought *rage*.
It brought *grief*.
It brought *a reckoning* I was not prepared for.

What made it worse was that the man who had stolen my identity was still alive. Still breathing. Still existing in the world… incarcerated, but unreachable. The truth sat between us, unresolved, waiting. There would be no immediate confrontation, no explanation, no accountability that night or the next.

Only the knowledge that he had taken my name, my lineage, and my truth, and that he had done it deliberately.

My biological father, the man whose blood I carried, was already gone.

That grief arrived differently. There would never be a chance to ask who he was or why he had left. No opportunity to see my face reflected back at me through time. I was grieving a man I had never known, while still living under the name of a man who had hurt me.

Professionals struggled with my response.

Some expected relief. Others framed my unraveling as instability, as if discovering your entire identity was built on a lie should be processed cleanly, efficiently, therapeutically.

But trauma does not respond to revelation the way logic expects.

Truth does not always **heal**. Sometimes it **destabilizes** everything you used to survive.

I wasn't mourning one loss. I was mourning many. The father I thought I had. The father I never met. The childhood that suddenly made sense in the worst way. The years I spent doubting myself because others told me I was wrong.

I had been right. And being right came at a cost.

I questioned my worth in ways I hadn't since childhood. If my name was a lie, what else was? If the abuse was tied to my identity, did that mean I had been marked from birth? I wrestled with thoughts I was ashamed to admit. Wondering if my existence itself had been a mistake, wondering if I had been born into harm.

No one prepares you for that kind of collapse.

There is no roadmap for grieving a truth that arrives decades too late. I carried it quietly, knowing that one day I would have to face the man who took my name, but not yet knowing how, when, or with whose support.

Finding out at thirty-five did not give me *peace*. It gave me **clarity**.

And it set the stage for a confrontation I never imagined I would have. One that would force me to speak directly to the man who claimed me in ink and hurt me in silence.

Chapter Seventeen

"Closure is not peace. Sometimes it is simply the end of pretending."

I was not okay after learning the truth.

People talk about truth as if it brings relief, as if knowing automatically sets you free. But this truth was different. The man who had abused me was also the man who had claimed me as his daughter. The man who signed my birth certificate. The man whose name I carried. And now I knew, with certainty, that he was not my father at all.

He was incarcerated for the abuse he caused. That was a relief, but it did not soften anything. If anything, it made what came next more complicated. I knew I could not face him alone.

So I worked with a victim services advocate, someone who met with me weekly, who helped me prepare for a confrontation I never imagined having. Each week, I wrote questions. Carefully. Deliberately. I printed photos, people I needed him to identify, pieces of a life I was trying to reconstruct.

This was not about forgiveness. It was about closure. Or at least, what I hoped closure might look like.

When the advocate met with him, he came back with words I will never forget. He told me that the man said, *"I've been trying to figure out how I was going to tell Millie the truth all these years."*

I remember staring at him, waiting for the rest of the sentence. Waiting for remorse. Waiting for accountability. Waiting for something that acknowledged what he had done.

Instead, he told me something else he had said. That when he got out, he couldn't wait for us to be a family again.

A family.

The word landed like a slap. Had he lost his mind?

A family? He wasn't even related to me. He had abused me. He had stolen my identity. He had destroyed whatever sense of safety I might have had, and now, years later, sitting behind bars, he spoke as if time had erased that truth.

That moment ignited a new kind of anger.

I was already furious. Furious that someone could harm children so deeply and then spend years incarcerated, protected from the world he damaged. Protected from bills.

Protected from daily survival. Protected from the weight of parenting, insurance, medical care, employment, housing, all the things I had been forced to navigate alone.

He did not have freedom. But he had shelter. And I had spent my life surviving in the open.

That injustice took time to come to terms with. I had to accept that the world does not balance harm the way we want it to. That consequences do not always feel proportional. That accountability, when it exists, does not undo damage.

But the hardest realization came later. It arrived quietly, after the rage settled into something colder. I realized that maybe I had been right all along. **He knew**.

He knew I felt like an outsider.
He knew I didn't look like him, because I didn't.
I looked like my mother.
And my mother had the affair.

I carried her face, her features, her reminder. And maybe that was why the distance felt deliberate. Why the hatred felt personal. Why I was treated differently in ways no one ever named.

He didn't just abuse me. He made sure I never belonged.

That knowledge rearranged my memories. It reframed the exclusion, the violence, the emotional cruelty. It wasn't random. It wasn't imagined.

It was informed. He knew the truth. And he let me grow up believing I was broken instead.

The confrontation did not give me peace. But it gave me clarity.

It told me that the ache I carried for decades, the feeling of being outside the circle, of never quite fitting, was not intuition gone wrong.

It was **recognition**. And with that recognition came something I had never had before: the ability to stop blaming myself.

Chapter Eighteen

"Some wounds don't bleed. They follow you on paper."

I still carry his last name.

The *man* who abused me.
The *man* who was never my father.
The *man* who knew the truth and let me live a **lie**.

His name is not mine, but it lives on my documents as if it is. It trails me everywhere, a reminder inked into records I cannot rewrite. It is on my identification. It is on legal forms. And worst of all, it is on my children's birth certificates.

My maiden name.

The name I handed to them without fully understanding what it carried.

There is something uniquely painful about seeing your abuser's name attached to your children, not because of blood, but because of bureaucracy. Because the system never asks whether a name is safe. It never asks whether it belongs.

It simply transfers it forward, as if harm does not echo through generations.

Every time I see it, it hurts.

Not in a sharp way. In a deep, settled way. Like a bruise that never quite fades. I think about how names are supposed to connect us to our history, our lineage, our people. Mine connects me to someone who stole my identity and used it to hurt me.

And I am still carrying it.

I wish I could say that learning the truth brought clarity to my relationships. It didn't. It complicated everything.

Meeting my biological siblings was not a single moment. It was a series of encounters shaped by timing, grief, and other people's wounds. Some welcomed me. Some kept their distance. Some said nothing at all.

Comments were made. *"What does she want?"*

That sentence lodged itself in my chest. What did I want?

I wanted **truth**.
I wanted **connection**.
I wanted to know **where** I came from.
I wanted to understand **why** I had always felt different.

But to them, my existence reopened something painful on my father's side of the family. They had their own stories. Their own grief. I was not just a sibling. I was evidence. A reminder. A living disruption to a narrative they had already survived.

I became the wound they did not want to touch.

Some siblings were kinder. Some welcomed me in ways I didn't know how to receive at first. We laughed. We shared stories. They helped when they could. And I clung to that connection, not because I was weak, but because I was starving.

Starving for **recognition**.
Starving for **resemblance**.
Starving for **proof** that I came from somewhere.

I saw echoes of the father I never met. A smile that felt familiar. A laugh that sounded like something my body remembered, even if my mind didn't. Being around them made the loss feel real, and briefly, survivable.

But even that relationship shifted. Not dramatically. *Quietly.*

We were born of the same man, but not of the same life.

Different *eras*.
Different *contexts*.
Different *expectations*.

I pray the door stays open... even just a crack. Because losing them would feel like losing my father all over again. And I don't know if I can carry that twice.

Then there were comments from the other side of my family. The one that still replays in my head. *"Well, at least you don't have to go around saying your daddy raped you now."*

As if *truth* erases **trauma**.
As if *blood* determines **harm**.
As if what happened to me needed genetic
confirmation to be **real**.

Those words gutted me.

They reduced years of abuse, confusion, and survival into something dismissible. They made it clear where I stood, not as a sister seeking connection, but as an inconvenience disrupting comfort.

That moment clarified something I had been avoiding.

Blood does not guarantee **belonging**. And truth does not guarantee **acceptance**.

I had spent much of my life trying to fit into families that could not hold me. First the one I was born into, then the one I was told was mine, and finally the one I discovered too late. Each time, I arrived hopeful. Each time, I learned that belonging is not automatic.

It is **chosen**.

The name I carry was never *chosen* by me.
The silence I endured was never *chosen* by me.
The fractures I inherited were never *chosen* by me.

And yet, I am still the one living with their weight.

I look at my children and feel both pride and grief. Pride that they have stability, safety, presence. Grief that their paperwork still carries a man who should have no claim to them at all.

I think about legacy… what we pass down, intentionally or not.

I cannot erase the name from the past. But I can decide what it means moving forward. I can teach my children that identity is not confined to documents. That love is not defined by blood. That truth matters, even when it costs you relationships.

I come from *broken lines*. But I am **not** broken.

I am building something new, not from inheritance, but from intention. And even though the reminders still hurt, even though the name still follows me, I know this:

What I create will matter more than what I was given.

Chapter Nineteen

"Some losses don't come alone. They arrive in waves."

The year I learned the truth about my identity was also the year I lost my brother on my mother's side of the family.

Those two events are forever linked in my body, truth and death arriving together, each undoing me in a different way. Just as I was trying to stand inside a reality I had never been prepared for, grief entered without asking.

My brother took his own life.

The call came on Christmas morning from the coroner's office. As if holidays were not already heavy enough. My children were in the middle of opening presents, laughter, and wrapping paper scattered around the room. I was trying to stay present for them, trying to hold the moment together, but I lost a piece of myself that day.

There are no words that make that sentence easier to carry. No version of it feels complete. His suicide cracked something open in me that had already been weakened by years of loss, distance, and unanswered questions. It felt like the ground gave way beneath what little stability I had left.

I drove to another state to clean out what remained of his life.

He had been living in a motel, not a place meant for living, but for disappearing. A twin bed. A sink. A small closet. An old built-in entertainment center at the foot of the bed. No private bathroom, only a shared one down the hall.

When I opened the door, the smell was unbearable.

His clothes were still on the floor where they had fallen when responders entered for the welfare check I had begged for. Alcohol bottles were everywhere. Pills scattered across surfaces, psychiatric medications and anti-drinking pills. Evidence that he had been trying.

Bed bugs crawled through everything. The bed was unmade. They moved through fabric and crevices as if they had always been there.

There was a dark stain on the carpet near the entrance, where his head had been.

I stood there, trying to breathe, trying to understand how someone I loved could be living like this without me fully knowing.

I picked up his phone.

Reading through his messages felt like discovering a second life… one he had never shown me. Conversations filled with pain he had kept hidden. Relationships I didn't know about. And then the messages that broke me completely.

He wrote that he couldn't bear living anymore.

In one message, he said he couldn't stand looking in the mirror. *Because he looked just like his abuser.*

That sentence still lives inside me.

In that moment, everything made sense in the worst way. The addiction. The isolation. The despair. The abuse had followed him into adulthood, reshaping how he saw himself, his body, his worth.

The people at the motel told me how kind he was. How gentle. How polite. They said they loved him. That he was always respectful, always thoughtful.

He showed the world one version of himself.

And carried another entirely alone.

Standing in that room, I felt the weight of every unanswered question. Every fractured relationship. Every moment, we were taught to endure instead of heal.

I loved my brother. I still do.

And I carry the truth of how he lived, and how he died, with me, not to sensationalize his pain, but to honor it. To say that his life mattered. That his suffering was real. That the conditions that shaped him were not his fault.

He was not *weak*. He was **wounded**.

And losing him changed me in ways I am still learning how to hold.

That same year, my youngest brother stepped out of my life, completely. Not suddenly. Not dramatically. Quietly.

I was always the one reaching out. Checking in. Sending messages. Asking how he was doing. It hurt in a way I struggled to explain—not because he was cruel, but because I never felt included. It always seemed there was no space for me in his life, no place where I fit naturally.

At the time, I took that pain personally.

Looking back now, I see something else.

He was building his life. He had a wife. A family. Responsibilities. He was trying to create stability… something none of us had been given growing up. Sometimes distance isn't rejection. Sometimes it's survival.

Still, understanding does not erase grief.

The system didn't just separate us physically when we were young. It fractured our ability to know each other as adults. It taught us how to live parallel lives instead of shared ones. We grew up without a foundation that might have carried us back to one another.

Over time, I lost connection to almost all of my younger siblings.

I think about them constantly. I think about their children, nieces, and nephews I have never met. Children whose lives unfold without me present. I wonder who they look like. I wonder what they love. I wonder if they ever ask about me.

I am not included in their lives.

I have never held their children. Never attended birthdays or holidays. Never been an aunt in the ways I imagined when we were younger. That absence aches in quiet, persistent ways.

And still, some instinct in me tries to protect them. Even now. Even from a distance.

I think about them when I hear sirens. When I see news stories. When something reminds me of how fragile life is. My body still reacts as if it is my job to keep them safe, even though they are not here, and I cannot reach them the way I once tried to.

So I pray for them. **Daily**.

Simple prayers that they are safe. That they are loved. That the damage does not keep traveling forward. But there was another weight I carried during that time, one that stayed hidden.

I was not free to live in my own truth.

After learning who my biological father was, I was asked, *explicitly and implicitly*, not to search for his family, not to reach out too far, not to disrupt what remained intact. They wanted their mother protected. They wanted her pain respected. And I understood that.

I truly did. *But* it cost me.

It meant holding my identity quietly once again. Knowing who I was, and still not being allowed to speak it freely. Discovering an entire side of myself and being asked to keep it contained, manageable, discreet.

I had lived most of my life in silence already. This felt like being asked to do it again.

I couldn't openly search for people who shared my blood. I couldn't ask questions the way someone else might. I couldn't explore where I came from without worrying about who it might hurt. Even in truth, I was still accommodating others before myself.

That made building relationships difficult, even with the siblings I did meet.

They were nearly forty years older than me.

They grew up in a different era, with a father I never knew and a life that looked nothing like mine. There was a generational gap that went beyond age, a difference shaped by decades I was never part of.

I don't blame them for that. But it made the connection fragile.

I often felt like I was stepping into a story already written, trying to find space for myself without disrupting what existed. Learning where I fit, and where I didn't, all over again.

Not being able to fully live in my truth made everything heavier.

It delayed healing. It complicated grief. It reinforced the feeling that my existence required careful handling—that my story was something to manage rather than something to honor.

I wondered if the distance from my siblings had something to do with my name.

With the fact that I don't share the same last name. With the truth surfacing so late and reshaping everything. If disowning me felt easier than holding the complexity of who I am and what my presence represents.

If that is true, I forgive them.

Not because it didn't hurt, but because I understand how heavy this story is. I understand the instinct to turn away when truth threatens stability. I don't blame them for choosing distance if that was the only way they knew how to survive.

The system did not just take our childhoods. It took our ability to reunite and authentically connect.

It took shared memory, shared repair, shared future. It left us trying to build lives without knowing how to find our way back to one another.

Losing my brother to suicide was devastating. Losing my siblings slowly, over time, has been its own kind of grief. And carrying truth without permission to live it fully made that grief lonelier still.

I carry all of this quietly, not because it doesn't matter, but because there is no one left to carry it with me. And yet, even in that solitude, I choose compassion over resentment.

For my *siblings*.
For *myself*.
For the *children* who grew up in a system that taught
us **separation** before it taught us **connection**.

I don't know if we will ever find our way back to each other.

But I know this: I have not stopped loving them. And I have not stopped hoping that somewhere, in ways I may never see, the damage ends with us.

Chapter Twenty

"There is a moment after the truth is spoken when the room goes quiet. Not because everything has been resolved, but because nothing else can be hidden."

I didn't anticipate how much silence would follow once I stopped carrying my story alone. I thought telling the truth would feel like release… like exhaling after holding my breath for decades. In some ways, it did. But it also left me standing in a new kind of stillness, one where the noise of survival no longer drowned out the question of what comes next.

Survival had always been my posture. My orientation to the world. I knew how to endure. I knew how to adapt. I knew how to stay upright in impossible conditions. What I didn't know, what no one had ever taught me, was how to live without bracing.

After everything was named, I realized something quietly devastating: I had never known who I was outside of surviving.

That realization didn't come with panic. It came with grief.

When your identity is shaped by crisis, stability can feel unfamiliar… even unsafe. There were moments when calm felt like a trap, when peace made me restless, when I found myself scanning for danger that never arrived. My body still remembered chaos as a language. Still expected loss to follow closeness. Still waited for the other shoe to drop.

Healing didn't erase that overnight. Instead, it asked me to slow down enough to notice it.

I began to understand that healing is not the absence of pain. It is the presence of choice. The choice to respond instead of react. The choice to stay instead of disappear. The choice to tell the truth without apologizing for its existence.

For the first time in my life, I wasn't being moved by someone else's decision. **I was choosing.**

That didn't mean everything became easy. Relationships didn't suddenly mend themselves. Family fractures didn't magically heal. Some people grew closer. Others stepped further away. There were doors that remained closed, no matter how gently I knocked.

I learned to stop measuring my worth by who stayed. That was one of the hardest lessons.

I had spent years believing that love required endurance. That if I just stayed quiet enough, flexible enough, forgiving enough, I could earn permanence. But healing demanded something different. It asked me to believe that I was allowed to take up space without proving my usefulness.

That I could be loved without performing survival.

Some days, that belief felt solid. Other days, it wavered. Healing is not linear. It circles back. It revisits old wounds from new angles. It surprises you with grief you thought you'd already processed and strength you didn't know you had.

I stopped chasing closure.

Closure implies an ending neat enough to wrap. My story doesn't offer that. What it offers instead is continuity... an understanding that I am still here, still growing, still allowed to change.

I stopped trying to reconcile everything that was taken.

Some losses don't get redeemed. Some injustices don't get corrected. Some questions don't receive answers. Accepting that was not surrender. It was clarity. It allowed me to stop fighting ghosts and start investing in what was real and present.

What survived after the telling was not *bitterness*. It was **discernment**.

I learned to recognize safety by how my body responded. I learned to trust discomfort as information, not weakness. I learned that boundaries are not walls. They are the architecture of self-respect.

Most importantly, I learned that my voice does not exist to convince anyone. **It exists to be true.**

I don't tell my story to be understood by everyone. I tell it so that silence no longer gets to decide who I am. I tell it because somewhere, someone is still standing in the place I once stood… confused, ashamed, convinced that survival is the same thing as living.

It isn't.

Living is **choosing yourself** even when no one claps.
Living is **staying present** when leaving would be easier.
Living is **allowing joy** without waiting for permission.

I am still learning how to do that.

There are days I get it wrong. Days I retreat. Days when old instincts flare up and try to take the wheel. But now, I notice. Now, I come back. Now, I don't disappear when things get hard.

That is what survived.

Not the *pain*.
Not the *labels*.
Not the *silence*.

I did. And that is enough to keep going.

PART 5

WHAT I HAD TO BUILD MYSELF

(Adulthood, survival skills, love, faith, and learning how to live without a map)

Chapter Twenty-One

"No one teaches you how to live when survival was your first language."

Adulthood did not arrive with *clarity*. It arrived with **bills**. With decisions that carried consequences I didn't yet understand. With responsibilities layered on top of unresolved pain. With the expectation that I would simply know how to function in a world I had never been prepared for.

I knew how to **endure**. I did not know how to *rest*.

I knew how to read danger in a room, how to stay alert, how to adapt quickly. I did not know how to trust calm, or how to believe that stability could last. When things were quiet, my body waited for disruption. When life slowed down, something in me tensed, ready.

Survival does not switch off just because circumstances improve.

There were no parents to call when something broke. No one to explain how credit worked, how leases worked, how mistakes followed you longer than you expected. I learned through error… often costly ones. Not because I was careless, but because guidance had never been modeled.

Every step forward felt like **risk**.

I didn't have a *safety net*.
No one to call if things went wrong.
No family to absorb mistakes.

Everything I had was fragile, dependent on momentum continuing forward.

That's how I ended up talking to someone on a plane.

It wasn't planned, just one of those conversations that happen in transit, when people share pieces of themselves because they believe they'll never see each other again. We talked about where we were from, where we were going. I didn't share much. I never did. But when the conversation turned toward logistics, where I was staying, what came next, I hesitated.

They offered help. A place to stay. Just temporarily.

I told myself it was practical. I told myself I was being resourceful. I told myself this was how adults navigated the world… accepting opportunities as they came.

At first, it seemed fine. Then the edges began to show.

Living in someone else's space reminded me how quickly power can shift when you need something. I watched myself become careful again. Quieter. More aware of moods. I returned to old habits without realizing it… making myself small, staying out of the way, minimizing my presence.

When the situation deteriorated, it didn't do so dramatically. There was no single argument or clear ending. Just tension. Discomfort. The unspoken understanding that I was no longer welcome.

I left with what I could carry. That's how homelessness happened… not as a sudden fall, but as a quiet slide.

I rotated between temporary places, telling myself it was short-term. I stayed with acquaintances just long enough not to wear out my welcome. I learned how to leave early and return late. How to avoid taking up space. How to make gratitude sound effortless.

Eventually, even those options disappeared.

Being homeless in a state where no one knew you is a particular kind of erasure. There is no history to lean on, no one who remembers you differently. You become invisible quickly, not because people don't see you, but because they don't know how to place you.

I learned how to blend into public spaces. How to stay alert without looking anxious. How to exist without drawing attention. I learned how to assess safety constantly… where I could rest, where I could go without being questioned, where I could disappear.

The hardest part wasn't the *instability*. It was the **confirmation**.

Being without a home felt like proof of something I had carried my entire life… that I was always meant to be temporary. That no matter how hard I worked or how far I traveled, I would always be on the margins, adjusting to spaces not designed to hold me.

I thought about how often I had been told I was *resilient, strong, independent.* None of those words helped when I was alone with nowhere to go.

I thought about school. The only place that had ever offered structure without expectation. I thought about how different things might have been if someone had noticed what I needed instead of praising how well I adapted.

Difference had followed me here, too.

My awareness of everything, the way environments shifted, the way people watched never shut off. Survival required constant attention.

I didn't feel *dramatic*. I felt **tired**.

Tired of **adjusting**.
Tired of **proving** I could manage.
Tired of **carrying** everything alone.

And still, I kept going.

I found my way back eventually, not because the system caught me, but because I caught myself. Because somewhere beneath the exhaustion, there was still a refusal to disappear completely.

This chapter of my life didn't teach me strength.

It taught me that visibility matters. That difference without support becomes vulnerability. That moving away doesn't resolve what was never acknowledged.

Home, I learned, is not something you can outrun your way into. It has to be **built**.

Or *chosen*.
Or *named*.
And I was still learning how to do that.

I learned how to work relentlessly, because work felt safer than stillness. Productivity became proof that I was doing life *"right."* If I stayed busy, maybe no one would notice how unsure I felt underneath it all.

But busyness is not stability.

And eventually, my body told the truth before my mind was ready to hear it. I burned out quietly.

Not in dramatic collapse, but in exhaustion that seeped into everything. Sleep became shallow. Decisions felt heavier. Small setbacks felt catastrophic. I didn't yet have language for nervous system overload or delayed development. I only knew that I was tired in a way rest didn't fix.

This was when I began to understand something important: Survival skills don't automatically translate into living skills.

Hyper-independence had kept me alive, but it also kept me isolated. Asking for help felt unnatural, almost dangerous. Depending on anyone, felt like inviting disappointment. I had learned early that needing less made me safer.

Unlearning that took time.

Relationships were the hardest part.

Love did not feel like refuge. It felt like exposure. Intimacy triggered memories I didn't always understand. Safety felt unfamiliar. Even kindness sometimes made me suspicious. I wanted connection deeply, but I didn't trust it to stay.

So I learned in fragments.

I learned how to *pause* instead of **reacting**.
How to notice when **fear**, not *reality*, was driving my decisions.
How to *sit with discomfort* without immediately trying to **escape** it.

I learned that boundaries were not rejection… they were structure. That saying no didn't make me ungrateful. That rest wasn't laziness. That I didn't have to earn the right to exist without pain.

These lessons came slowly.

Often, through therapy, I didn't know I needed until my late twenties. Through conversations that scared me. Through moments of choosing honesty, even when silence would have been easier.

And through parenting.

Becoming a parent forced me to confront everything I had normalized. I couldn't teach my children emotional regulation if I didn't practice it myself. I couldn't model safety if I didn't believe it was possible. They needed more than my survival… they needed my presence.

That changed me.

I began to build routines not out of control, but out of care. I paid attention to how my body responded to stress. I learned to recognize triggers without shame. I started asking myself different questions. Not *"What's wrong with me?"* But *"What happened to me, and what do I need now?"*

This was not healing as an event. It was healing as maintenance.

As *practice*.
As *repetition*.
As *choosing differently*, again and again, even when
the old patterns whispered louder.

I did not suddenly feel whole. But I began to feel grounded. And that was enough to keep building.

Chapter Twenty-Two

"Healing doesn't only happen in therapy. Sometimes it happens in the way you stock your pantry and lock your front door."

There are parts of adulthood that people learn without realizing they learned them.

They learn because someone showed them. Because there was a parent in the next room who made dinner every night, even when they were tired. Because there was a grandfather who taught them how to change a tire. Because there was an aunt who explained what *"interest"* meant before they signed anything. Because there was a family table where bills were discussed out loud, not hidden in drawers like shame.

I did not have that.

I had instinct. I had fear. I had a nervous system trained to anticipate loss and the certainty of never doing anything right. And I had an internal rule I didn't even know I was obeying: **don't break or fail, no matter what it costs.**

So when I stepped fully into building a life, I didn't start with dreams. I started with triage.

Housing.
Food.
Safety.
Consistency.

Four walls that didn't change. A place where I could exhale without listening for footsteps. A refrigerator that wasn't an insult, either empty or filled with things I wasn't allowed to touch. A front door that locked and stayed locked. A space that didn't feel borrowed.

I didn't realize how much of my body had been living as if the floor could drop out at any moment until I finally had a floor that didn't move.

At first, stability felt like a trick.

When you grow up in chaos, peace can feel suspicious. Calm can feel like the quiet before something breaks. A normal day can make you uneasy because your body is conditioned to expect that **"normal"** never lasts. Even after I created a life that looked stable from the outside, I would catch myself waiting, *braced, scanning*, like I was only renting the calm.

The smallest things could trigger it.

A delayed phone call.
A short text.
A change in tone.
A bill I didn't expect.
A car making a sound it hadn't made before.

My mind would start running calculations: *How bad could this get? How fast would it fall apart? What would I do if it did?*

I didn't call it *anxiety* back then. I called it **being responsible**. But it wasn't *responsibility*. It was **hypervigilance** dressed as competence.

I learned quickly that adult life punishes ignorance, even when that ignorance is inherited.

No one teaches you how credit works if your childhood taught you that everything you love can be taken without warning. No one shows you how to build savings when you spent your youth learning to hoard peace in ten-second increments. No one explains that missing a payment can follow you for years when the system that raised you operated on a different kind of consequence... instant, physical, unpredictable.

I made mistakes. Not because I didn't care. Because I was learning a language I had never been taught.

And every mistake felt catastrophic, not because of the money, but because of what it activated in me: the old belief that one wrong move could cost me everything.

Sometimes I would stare at paperwork until the words blurred, my chest tight, my throat thick with a panic I couldn't justify. The form was simple. The task was ordinary. But my body didn't experience it as ordinary. My body experienced it as risk. As exposure. As the possibility of being told, — *again,* —that I didn't deserve to be here.

This is what people don't understand when they say, *"You're so strong."*

They think strength is a personality trait.

They don't see the trembling under the surface. They don't see the calculations. They don't see how *"strong"* often means alone.

And I was tired of being alone.

Not in a dramatic, collapsing way. In a quiet, constant way that seeped into everything. The kind of tired that comes from being your own parent and your own safety net and your own reassurance all at once.

I wanted to be held.

Not *fixed*.
Not *saved*.
Just **held**.

But holding requires **trust**. And trust, for me, *was never free*. It had always been a risk assessment.

Even when people were kind, I watched for the catch. I waited for kindness to turn into expectation. I waited for love to become leverage. I waited for the moment I would be told I was too much, too complicated, too dramatic.

So I stayed useful.

I cooked.
I cleaned.
I helped.
I anticipated.
I overfunctioned.

Usefulness was the version of love I understood, because in my early life, being easy was the closest thing I had to being safe. But adulthood began to demand something deeper than usefulness.

At some point, a life built purely on survival becomes unlivable. Not because it collapses publicly, but because you can feel yourself disappearing inside it. You become capable, productive, efficient, while the part of you that is human stays starved.

That starvation doesn't always look like **sadness**.

Sometimes it looks like *numbness*.
Sometimes it looks like *irritability* that doesn't match the moment.
Sometimes it looks like **a woman standing in her own kitchen, surrounded by evidence of a life she fought to build, and still feeling like she could vanish without anyone noticing**.

I reached a point where I could no longer pretend that competence was enough. So I started building differently.

Not *perfectly*.
Not *quickly*.
But **deliberately**.

I built routines... small, grounded things that didn't depend on mood.

Waking up at the same time.
Making coffee the same way.
Folding laundry while music played.
Stocking the pantry before it ran empty.
Keeping extra soap under the sink.

Buying two tubes of toothpaste so I would never experience that particular kind of scarcity again.

It sounds *small*. But for me, it wasn't *small*. It was **corrective**.

Each routine was a message my nervous system had never received: *You are allowed to prepare for comfort. You are allowed to assume you'll still be here tomorrow.*

And then there was the deeper kind of building, the kind that doesn't show up in cabinets and calendars. The building of **boundaries**.

I didn't grow up with *boundaries*.
I grew up with **rules**.
Rules are *imposed*. Boundaries are **chosen**.
Rules taught me *compliance*.
Boundaries taught me **self-respect**.

At first, boundaries felt cruel.

Saying no felt like **betrayal**.
Disagreeing felt like **danger**.
Asking for what I needed felt like **demanding** something I hadn't earned.

I had to learn, *slowly*, that a boundary is not an attack. It is a structure. It is the frame of a life that doesn't collapse every time someone else becomes disappointed.

I practiced in small ways.

I didn't answer texts immediately.
I let someone be upset with me without rushing to fix it.
I stopped apologizing for existing.
I said, *"I can't,"* and let that be a full sentence.

The first time I did it, my body reacted like I had committed a crime. My heart raced. My hands went cold. I felt sick. I almost took it back just to make the discomfort stop.

But I didn't. And the world didn't end.

That was the beginning of a new education, one no caseworker had ever offered, no program had ever taught: the education of safety.

Safety isn't just locks and alarms and a stable address. Safety is knowing that you can be honest and still be loved. Safety is having relationships where your nervous system doesn't have to stay on patrol. Safety is being allowed to be messy and still be held.

I didn't know how to receive that. Receiving was harder than giving.

Giving felt active. Giving felt controlled. Giving let me stay in the role I understood… provider, helper, anchor. But receiving, required vulnerability. It required admitting that I needed. And I had built my identity around not needing.

So I resisted it.

Even when people offered care, I minimized. I said I was fine. I changed the subject. I folded the offering into something neat and manageable, like I planned to use it later.

Later rarely came. Because later, always felt unsafe.

It took time to realize that my refusal to receive wasn't independence. It was **fear**.

Fear that if I took something, *it could be taken back.*
Fear that if I let someone close, *they could leave.*
Fear that if I admitted what I needed, *I would be judged for it.*

Sometimes I could feel the old child in me watching.

Waiting.
Suspicious.
Prepared to be disappointed.

And sometimes, I was disappointed. Not because people were cruel. Because people are people.

Some relationships couldn't hold my story. Some couldn't hold my boundaries. Some preferred the version of me that was endlessly accommodating, endlessly forgiving, endlessly quiet.

That loss **hurt**. But it also *clarified*.

There is a grief that comes with realizing not everyone deserves access to you. Not everyone deserves the most tender parts of your life. Grief, because you want love to be simple. Grief, because you want belonging to be automatic. Grief, because you still carry that longing for a family that stays.

But clarity is a form of protection.

I began to understand that peace is not found by shrinking. Peace is found by choosing environments that don't require your disappearance.

That choice mattered most when I became a parent.

Parenting put my healing into motion in real time, in the middle of daily life, where triggers don't announce themselves, and you can't pause the world to process.

My children didn't need *my perfection*. They needed my **presence**.

And presence required that I stop living in a constant state of internal evacuation… half in the past, half braced for the future, rarely fully here.

They needed me to **stay**. So I learned what it meant to stay.

To breathe through discomfort instead of escaping it.
To admit when I was overwhelmed without turning it into shame.
To apologize when I got it wrong… not to grovel, not to erase myself, but to model repair.

That was new.

In my childhood, conflict didn't end in repair. It ended in silence. It ended in consequences. It ended in pretending nothing happened while your body still carried the imprint of what did.

With my children, I wanted something else. I wanted them to know:

That **love** could handle *truth*.
That **emotions** weren't *threats*.
That **being upset** didn't mean being *abandoned*.

But teaching that meant practicing it.

And practicing it meant confronting parts of myself I had survived by burying.

Sometimes my child would cry, and something in me would tense, not because their tears were wrong, but because tears had never been safe in my early life. Tears had invited attention, and attention had not meant comfort.

So I retrained my body. I would kneel down, breathe, soften my voice, and remind myself: *This is not then.* **This is now.**

My child *is not my past.*
Their feelings *are not a threat.*
Their needs *do not endanger me.*

And I would hold them anyway. Not because it came naturally. Because I refused to let my history be the architect of their nervous system.

That refusal became a kind of devotion. Not a loud one. Not performative. A daily, quiet devotion made of choices most people never have to think about.

Choosing gentleness when your body learned
survival.

Choosing patience when your childhood taught
urgency.
Choosing consistency when your early life was built
on **rupture**.

There were days I felt proud. Days I felt haunted. Days I felt both at once.

There were moments I looked at my children and felt a grief so sharp it surprised me—a grief for what they were receiving that I had never been given. Not because I begrudged them, but because the contrast was undeniable.

Sometimes the grief arrived in ordinary places.

Standing in the grocery store, watching a mother laugh with her daughter, and feeling something tighten in my chest. Sitting at a school event, seeing families clustered together, and realizing, *again,* that no one was there for me the way I was there for my children. Hearing someone talk about calling their mom for advice, and feeling that old ache open like a seam.

I didn't always know what to do with that grief. So I let it exist.

That was part of healing, too. Allowing the feelings to have a place without turning them into shame or self-pity. Allowing the truth to be true: it hurts. And also: *I'm here*.

I began to understand that healing isn't a destination where you arrive and suddenly everything makes sense.

Healing is a *practice*. A **maintenance**.

A series of choices repeated so often they begin to rewrite your instincts. And one of the most important choices I made, *again and again*, was this:

I stopped building my life around proving I was okay. I started building it around being honest about what I needed.

That honesty didn't make me *weaker*. It made me **real**.

It made *room for people* who could hold the truth
without turning away.
It made *room for relationships* that didn't require my
performance.
It made *room for joy* that wasn't followed
immediately by guilt.

And slowly, so slowly I didn't notice it at first, my body began to believe me. It began to settle.

Not completely. Not permanently. Trauma doesn't vanish because you want it to. But it softened. The alarms didn't blare as often. The panic didn't hijack every moment. I found pockets of calm that didn't feel like traps.

I began to recognize what safety felt like not as an idea, but as a sensation.

Shoulders unclenching.
Breath deepening.
Sleep coming without bargaining.
Laughter rising without monitoring the room.

These were the things I had to build myself. Not because I was special. Because I had to.

And in building them, I started to understand something that changed the way I saw my life: I wasn't just surviving anymore. I was learning how to belong... to my body, to my home, to my children, to a future that didn't require my disappearance.

That learning wasn't glamorous.

It didn't look like a breakthrough scene in a movie. It looked like waking up and choosing softness anyway. Choosing honesty anyway. Choosing to stay anyway.

It looked like building a life not from inheritance, but from intention. And for the first time, I could feel something I had rarely felt before… not pride, not performance, not relief.

Something *quieter*.
Something *steadier*.
Hope.

Not the kind of hope that denies reality. The kind of hope that comes from realizing you can live inside reality and still make something good.

I didn't get a foundation. So I became one. And that, more than anything, was the beginning of a life that wasn't just endured.

It was *lived*.

Chapter Twenty-Three

*"Safety was never something I learned by feeling it.
I learned it by managing around its absence."*

Growing up, food was not flexible. It was controlled, rationed, and ritualized. There were too many children, too little money, and no room for preference. We did not eat out, not ever. Restaurants were not just unaffordable; they were unthinkable. I remember the embarrassment of paper food stamps, the way my body tensed in checkout lines, the awareness of being seen. Hunger carried shame, and shame trained silence.

At home, every meal came with rules.

You ate what was on your plate.
You did not drink your milk until your food was
gone.
Milk was served with every dinner, regardless of
whether it paired with the meal or your body
tolerated it.

If you didn't finish, your plate waited for you, **cold**, at the next mealtime. And the next. Until it was gone.

Food was not *nourishment*. It was **compliance**.

There was no listening to appetite. No learning hunger cues, fullness, or preference. There was only obedience. Eating became transactional: endure now so the consequence doesn't stretch longer. I learned early how to override my body, how to disconnect from discomfort, how to treat physical signals as irrelevant when they conflicted with authority.

Those lessons didn't stay in childhood.

When I entered foster care, food looked different, but it was still controlled. Meals were planned. Snacks were scheduled. Portions were decided by someone else. Even kindness came with structure. Even abundance had rules. You ate when it was time. You took what was given. You did not ask for more unless it was allowed.

I developed tastes quietly, certain textures, certain flavors I gravitated toward, but access was inconsistent. There was no pantry freedom. No opening the fridge just because you wanted something. Wanting itself felt inappropriate. I learned to adapt my appetite to availability rather than need.

By the time I reached adulthood, food carried more meaning than sustenance ever should have.

Food became comfort long before it became a concern. Eating was the one thing that soothed me when nothing else did. I never learned to see myself as beautiful. No one praised me for it, no one told me I was enough. That absence settled into my body. Comfort came quietly, in bites and rituals meant to replace what I never received.

When I was finally allowed to choose. When no one was watching, no one controlling, no one enforcing rules. I ate freely. Not recklessly, but insistently. I ate what I wanted, when I wanted, because I could. Because no one could take it away. Because permission itself felt like safety.

That freedom mattered. But it came with consequences my body would eventually have to carry.

Years of disregarding hunger cues, forcing consumption, pairing food with stress instead of care, those patterns showed up later as health issues. Digestive problems. Inflammation. A body confused by decades of mixed messages. I had to relearn what hunger actually felt like. I had to separate nourishment from survival. I had to teach myself that eating did not need to be urgent, defensive, or emotional to be valid.

Healing wasn't about **restriction**. It was about *trust*.

Learning to trust that food would be there tomorrow. That I didn't have to finish everything in front of me to be safe. That my body was allowed to say yes and no without punishment. That fullness was not failure.

That work took time. It also coincided with another realization: I had always worked. I had never not worked. But I never felt ahead.

Money, like food, has always been something I managed carefully and rarely felt secure around. I learned early how to get by. How to stretch. How to prioritize needs over wants. How to survive without margin. Saving felt theoretical. Something other people did. Something that required excess, I had never known how to access.

Even now, adulthood has not erased that pattern entirely.

I work. I contribute. I pay my bills. And still, there is rarely a sense of being ahead. Only of being okay. Of being stable enough. Of having needs met.

And I've made peace with that. Because here is the truth I hold carefully and without shame:

I *am* healthy now.
My children *are* safe.
We *have* food.

THE LIE THAT NAMED ME

We *have* shelter.
We *have* consistency.

I am **not** homeless.
I am **not** lost to addiction.
I am **not** incarcerated.
I am **not** invisible.
I am **not** the monster the system quietly prepares the
world to expect.

There is a narrative attached to children who grow up in
care. We are broken, volatile, destined for failure. That if we
struggle, it is inevitable. That if we succeed, it is exceptional.
Both assumptions dehumanize us.

I **did not** fail because I wasn't *adopted*.
I **was not** unchosen because I was *defective*.
I **was not** hard to love because I was inherently *difficult*.

I was a child shaped by scarcity, silence, and survival. And
I am an adult who learned *slowly, imperfectly* how to build
safety where it had never existed before. My life may not look
impressive on paper.

But it is *steady*.
It is *intentional*.
It is *mine*.

I no longer measure success by how far ahead I am.

I measure it by how **regulated** my body feels.
By how **safe** my children are.
By how rarely fear drives my decisions now.

Learning safety did not come all at once.

It came through groceries bought *without panic*.
Through meals eaten *without urgency*.
Through permission to rest *without guilt*.

Through understanding that stability is not flashy, it is quiet, repetitive, and earned over time.

I am not behind. I am rebuilding from a starting line that was moved without my consent.

And today, that rebuilding looks like nourishment without punishment, work without self-erasure, and a life that no longer revolves around proving I survived.

I already did.

Chapter Twenty-Four

"Love doesn't erase trauma. It asks you to meet it honestly."

My marriage has not been easy.

I love my husband deeply, but loving him required learning what a healthy marriage actually is. Not the idea of one. Not the image people present. The real, imperfect, sometimes uncomfortable work of two people trying to build something without having been shown how.

We still argue.
We still fight.

There is no fairy tale here. And that matters, because pretending otherwise would erase the work it took to get where we are.

Being intimate was hard for me in ways I didn't fully understand at first. My body carried memories my mind had learned to compartmentalize. Touch was not neutral. Vulnerability did not feel safe. Even love sometimes felt like exposure.

Trust had to be practiced.

Not *assumed*.
Not *rushed*.
Practiced.

I had to learn how to share space with someone who had not lived my life. Someone who didn't know the details of my past, who hadn't grown up adapting to danger, who didn't automatically read rooms the way I did. Loving him meant learning how to explain myself instead of expecting him to already understand.

That was harder than I expected.

I had spent so much of my life surviving quietly that sharing my story felt like reopening wounds rather than healing them. Explaining why certain things triggered me. Why raised voices made my body react before my thoughts could catch up. Why silence sometimes felt safer than conversation.

I had to learn how to let someone see all of that without assuming it would make them leave.

We had to learn each other. *Slowly. Intentionally.*

We became friends before we became strong partners. We learned how to laugh together, how to sit in silence together, how to come back to one another after disagreements instead of retreating into old patterns. Love, for us, became something built, not inherited.

My husband has his own struggles.

And sometimes those struggles retrigger parts of my childhood trauma. There were moments when I had to learn how to love him where he was, while still protecting myself. Boundaries were not rejection. They were necessary.

We did not have role models to look up to.

Neither of us came from homes where healthy relationships were demonstrated consistently. We were figuring it out in real time, learning through mistakes, adjusting when something didn't work, choosing again when walking away would have been easier.

Being intentional became our anchor.

We had to decide, again and again, not to hurt each other just because we were hurt. To pause instead of react. To listen instead of defend. To stay curious instead of shutting down.

That didn't come naturally. We lost people along the way.

Friends who left because we chose each other. People who didn't understand why we set boundaries. Relationships that couldn't survive our growth. That loss hurt, but it clarified something important: choosing your marriage sometimes means disappointing others.

Counseling played a role in our survival.

Not because we were broken, but because we were learning. We needed language for conflict. Tools for communication. A space where neither of us had to be the expert. Counseling helped us understand that struggle does not mean failure… it means engagement.

Marriage taught me something I didn't expect.

That love doesn't demand *perfection*.
It demands **presence**.

I didn't need someone to save me. I needed someone willing to stay while I learned how to trust.

We are still *learning*.
Still *choosing* each other.
Still *growing*.

Our marriage is not proof that trauma disappears. It is proof that healing can happen alongside someone, not because they fix you, but because they are willing to walk with you honestly.

And that, for me, has been *enough*.

176

Chapter Twenty-Five

"I love my children in ways that scare me."

Becoming a mother didn't heal my past. It exposed it. I didn't realize how much fear I was carrying until I had something to lose that I loved more than my own life. From the moment I held my child, something shifted inside me… not softly, not gently, but with force. Love arrived fully formed and immediately followed by terror.

I was responsible now. Not just for survival, but for safety.

My childhood had taught me that loss doesn't announce itself. It arrives quietly, without warning, without fairness. People disappear. Homes vanish. Lives fracture. I had lived long enough knowing that nothing is guaranteed, and suddenly I was responsible for protecting someone who trusted me completely.

That weight settled deep in my body.

I watched my children sleep and checked their breathing longer than necessary. I stood in doorways long after bedtime, my chest tight, not only with worry, but with awe.

They existed. I had built a family. That fact alone still feels miraculous to me. And sometimes my fear moved faster than the moment I was in, scanning for danger even when everything was fine.

I told myself it was *love*. Sometimes, it was **fear**. Before any of that, I was told I would never have children.

Doctors explained it clinically, tracing the damage back to abuse my body endured long before it had language for pain. I listened the way I had learned to listen to bad news… quietly, without protest. Inside, I was devastated.

Motherhood was never a casual dream for me. It was a vision I carried for years. A chance to build something safe, to give what I never received, to create a family rooted in presence instead of fear. Being told that might never happen felt like another theft layered onto so many others.

I miscarried twice.

Those losses were private and heavy. Grief folded inward because I didn't know how to ask for comfort around something that already felt like failure. My body felt unreliable, as if it had betrayed me on top of everything else. Fertility treatments followed… pills, schedules, waiting, hope measured in cycles.

After a year, I gave up.

Not dramatically. *Quietly*. I told myself it was safer not to want something that might never come. Letting go felt like protection.

And then, against expectation, against fear, I had my daughters. Even *joy* came with **grief**.

Someone had hurt me so deeply that for years, I believed my dream of being a mother might never happen. Holding my girls, I felt gratitude and rage intertwined. Love so powerful it scared me, and anger for what had almost been taken.

Parenting, I learned quickly, is a constant reckoning.

There are moments I am not proud of. Times I have raised my voice. Times fear reached my reactions before patience did. Times my past leaked into the present in ways I didn't intend. I have made mistakes.

But I have never abused my children. That distinction matters.

I parent with an awareness that is sometimes heavy. I am constantly balancing. Trying not to parent from the raw edges of my trauma, trying not to let fear disguise itself as control. I wanted to give my children what I never had: a sense of safety that didn't depend on silence. A home that didn't disappear. A childhood that didn't require adaptation to survive.

But I didn't have a model for that. I was building something I had never seen. And I was terrified of failing.

I didn't just fear losing my children *physically*. I feared losing them *emotionally*.

Losing their trust.
Losing their sense of safety in the world.
Becoming too much, or not enough.

Sometimes I caught it happening in real time. I would feel myself tighten when one of my children pulled away. I would react more strongly than the moment required. I would want reassurance from them that everything was okay. That we were okay. And then the shame would follow, sharp and immediate.

They were not responsible for my fear. *I was.*

Parenting forced me to confront how deeply my past still lived in my body. Trauma doesn't disappear when you love harder. It shows up where love feels most vulnerable.

I had to learn how to pause. How to *breathe*. How to separate past danger from present reality. That did not come naturally.

There were moments when fear almost won. When my instinct was to pull my children closer instead of letting them grow. When protection threatened to become a cage. I had to learn that safety isn't created by eliminating risk, but by teaching resilience and trust.

That lesson was painful.

I wanted certainty. Guarantees. Proof that if I did everything right, nothing bad would happen. But parenting does not offer that. It demands surrender in ways I wasn't prepared for.

So I **grieved**.

I grieved the childhood I didn't have.
The safety I never learned.
The illusion that I could prevent all harm if I just
tried hard enough.

What I could do was different.

I could *show up*.
I could *listen*.

I could *repair* when I got it wrong.

I learned how to apologize to my children, not as weakness, but as promise. I learned how to name my emotions instead of letting them leak into my reactions. I learned that breaking cycles doesn't mean never failing… it means noticing, correcting, and staying present.

I have probably spoiled my children.

People have judged me for that. For my choices. For the way I sometimes move into full protection mode. But children need advocates. Sometimes parents must be the voice their child does not yet have.

No one was that for me.

I never wanted my children to grow up believing they had to take care of me. I never wanted them to feel responsible for my healing, my emotions, my past. That boundary matters to me deeply.

They sometimes think it's strange that I watch them sleep.

No matter how old they get, I still stand in doorways, watching their chests rise and fall. Not just from worry, but from awe. They are my everything.

I want them to *know their worth* without earning it.

To *dream* without fear of punishment.
To *believe* they matter simply because they exist.

They see me struggle. And that is okay.

They see effort. Repair. Honesty.

They see that love is not perfection; it is accountability.

And so I write this for them:

A letter to my children

I love you in ways that don't always look calm.

There are moments I watch you breathe while you sleep and feel my chest tighten, not from worry alone, but from awe. You exist in a world I tried to build differently from the one I grew up in. You move through spaces with a confidence I didn't have, and sometimes I have to remind myself not to confuse fear with protection.

I am learning as I go.

There will be moments when I hold on too tightly. When my voice sharpens because fear gets there before patience. When my past leaks into the present in ways I don't intend. When that happens, I need you to know this:

You are not responsible for my history.
You are not here to heal me.
You are not here to carry what I carried.

You are here to be children. To grow. To question. To leave and come back and leave again if you need to.

If I ever apologize to you, it is not because I am weak. It is because I want you to know repair is possible. That love does not disappear when mistakes are named. That safety can include honesty.

You are my proof that cycles can be interrupted.

And if fear ever makes me quiet when I should speak, I hope you forgive me – and then speak anyway.

Parenting did not erase my trauma. But it gave me purpose.

It gave me reason to choose differently. To pause. To repair. To stay present even when fear whispers louder than trust.

Love, when practiced intentionally, became something stronger than fear.

And that is the legacy I am building… without a map, but with intention.

Chapter Twenty-Six

"Belief is not obedience when it refuses to look away."

Faith entered my life before I understood what it was asking of me.

When I was a child, church was not a choice. It was a ritual. One layered with confusion and contradiction. Every Sunday, we boarded a church bus while our parents stayed home. We went without them, sat in pews without explanation, learned songs and scriptures without context. I watched other children arrive with families who seemed united by belief, while we arrived alone, dropped off, and collected later like participants in something no one bothered to explain.

I didn't understand what faith was supposed to mean in a house where harm was constant.

Scripture was handed to us freely. Bible verses were quoted often. Prayer was expected. And yet, the God being spoken about did not seem to intervene in the places where we needed protection most. I learned early how disorienting it is to be told about love and mercy while living inside fear.

We weren't allowed to dress how we wanted. We weren't allowed to cut our hair. Control was disguised as righteousness, and obedience was framed as virtue. I absorbed these messages quietly, unsure which rules belonged to God and which belonged to the people who hurt us.

When I was around nine years old, I attended a church event with a neighbor. I remember going to the altar and saying the sinner's prayer. I didn't fully understand what I was saying, only that it felt important... that it mattered. Faith, even then, felt less like certainty and more like reaching for something that might hold.

When I was thirteen, everything shifted.

My abuser moved the five of us into an apartment. It was my freshman year of high school, and overnight, I became the oldest in a way that had nothing to do with age. I became the caretaker. The organizer. The emotional container for what no one else would hold. We still went to church. I was baptized around that time. I remember it clearly because my hand was in a cast.

During the years I was in the system, from thirteen to eighteen, church became more than routine. I attended services, youth groups, and events. I volunteered. I saved money to attend a faith-based internship. I didn't realize then how much I was reaching for structure, for meaning, for something that suggested my life wasn't random.

When I was taken away again at fourteen, I knew, **deeply**, that I would never have a family in the way other people did.

Faith didn't fix that knowledge. But it sat with me inside it.

It wasn't until my thirties that I understood how much my faith had mattered, not because it answered my questions, but because it kept me alive. Faith, for me, had never been about certainty. It had been about endurance. About finding something, **anything,** that suggested suffering wasn't meaningless, even when it went unanswered.

Community, however, remained difficult.

Even now, walking into church can be triggering. Trauma doesn't disappear in sacred spaces. Sometimes it sharpens. Sitting among families, listening to language about obedience and forgiveness, I feel my body brace. Faith has always been personal for me... private, cautious, shaped by lived experience rather than doctrine.

After the losses, prayer changed.

It felt awkward. Unnecessary. Almost dangerous. I didn't know what to ask for anymore. Nothing I wanted could be fixed. Nothing I had lost could be returned. So I stopped praying the way I had been taught.

Instead, I sat in silence.

Sometimes anger rose up sharp, unfiltered. Not the kind you soften with polite theology, but the kind that asks why suffering keeps finding the same people. *Why children learn pain before safety. Why loss accumulates in lives that have already carried too much.*

I didn't say those thoughts out loud.

I had spent too long learning which truths were acceptable. Even in faith spaces, I felt pressure to behave… to be grateful, hopeful, composed. I knew how to play that role well.

But inside, something was unraveling.

I began to notice how easily belief can become another form of silence. *How often people reach for faith to avoid sitting with discomfort. How often God is used to explain things no one actually wants to understand.*

I didn't want *explanations*. I wanted **acknowledgment**.

I wanted someone, *anyone*, to say this was too much. That anger made sense. That grief didn't mean weakness or lack of faith.

I didn't hear that. So I stayed anyway.

Not because staying felt right, but because leaving felt like severing the last thread of meaning I had. I didn't have family to fall back on. I didn't have a home that held me when things fell apart. Faith, imperfect and incomplete, became a place where I could sit with questions without being abandoned entirely.

I wasn't *comforted*. But I was **present**.

That mattered more than I understood at the time.

Grief didn't fade in the years that followed. It shifted. Some days it lived quietly in the background. Other days it surfaced unexpectedly… a memory, a thought, a moment that reopened everything.

It changed how I loved.

I became cautious with my heart, even as I longed for connection. I searched for permanence in places that couldn't offer it. I wanted assurance that people would stay, that love wouldn't dissolve without warning.

That longing followed me into motherhood.

Loving my children reopened everything. Love felt overwhelming… beautiful, terrifying. Fear lived alongside it constantly: fear of loss, fear of repetition, fear that history might reach forward and touch them too. I had to learn, daily, how to loosen my grip. How to let love be expansive instead of controlling.

Faith grew quieter then.

Less about *answers*.
More about **grounding**.
Less about *certainty*.
More about **presence**.

I didn't trust easily… not people, not systems, not even God. Trust had never been modeled as safe. It had always come with conditions.

So I practiced a different kind of faith.

One that didn't require *pretending*.
One that allowed **anger** to exist alongside *belief*.
One that made room for **doubt** without *shame*.

I stopped expecting faith to *fix things*. I started allowing it to **witness them**.

That shift didn't heal everything. It didn't erase the past. But it gave me space to exist honestly. To admit when things hurt, when I was afraid, when I didn't know what came next.

For someone who had spent her life adapting to survive, that honesty felt radical.

I didn't rebuild my life all at once. I built it slowly, unevenly, sometimes reluctantly. I learned that endurance doesn't always look strong. Sometimes it looks like staying when leaving would be easier. Sometimes it looks like refusing to numb yourself even when feeling hurts.

Faith didn't rescue me. But it stayed.

And in a life where home was never guaranteed, where truth was often dangerous, and where love came with conditions, that presence, *imperfect, unresolved, honest,* mattered more than certainty ever could.

Chapter Twenty-Seven

"Family is not a title you assign. It is a relationship you earn."

The word *family* has never landed softly in my body.

For most people, it is warm. Comforting. A given. For me, it is layered with loss, confusion, and expectations that were never met. It carries memories of being taken, renamed, reassigned, and told to belong before I ever felt safe enough to choose it.

As a child in foster care, I hated being told to call someone *"Mom."*

I didn't hate the people themselves. I hated the demand. The assumption. The pressure wrapped in something that was supposed to feel nurturing. Being told to call a stranger Mom after being ripped from a home, no matter how broken that home was, felt like a betrayal of reality.

It felt like false hope.

You don't replace a mother by title.
You don't erase grief by renaming it.

And you don't build trust by demanding intimacy.

I watched adults insist that children call them Mom or Dad as if language alone could heal displacement. As if the word itself could do the work of safety, consistency, and time. It unsettled me, not because I didn't want connection, but because connection cannot be forced.

Children in care have already lost enough.

They have lost their people.
Their routines.
Their sense of continuity.

To then ask them to perform belonging, to speak it before they feel it, creates a kind of emotional dissonance that lingers. It teaches children to pretend. To comply. To mirror expectations instead of listening to their own readiness.

I needed *time*.
I needed *choice*.
I needed *honesty*.

And I needed permission to let family mean something different.

For a long time, the word *family* felt like something I had failed at. Something I didn't get because I wasn't good enough, quiet enough, adoptable enough. It felt like a door that had closed permanently, leaving me to figure out life without a blueprint others inherited without realizing it.

Eventually, I had to grieve that.

I had to accept that I would never have what most people consider a traditional family. No parents to return to. No holidays that felt rooted. No inherited stories or shared childhood memories told around a table.

That grief was necessary.

Because once I stopped trying to force my life into a shape it would never take, something else became possible.

I began to choose.

Family, I learned, is not something assigned by paperwork or proximity. It is not guaranteed by blood or titles. Family is built slowly, through presence and consistency. Through showing up without obligation. Through staying when it would be easier to leave.

I have people in my life who feel like family.

Mentors who guided me when no one else did. Adults who offered stability without claiming ownership.

People who didn't demand intimacy but earned trust over time.

I don't call them Mom or Dad. But they matter.

They are my chosen family. People who walked beside me without needing to replace anyone, people who respected the complexity of my history instead of trying to overwrite it.

I also had to expand my definition even further. I consider the children still moving through the system, my family.

The kids searching for *safety*.
The ones adapting quietly.
The ones labeled *difficult* or *invisible*.

They are my siblings in a way that doesn't require introduction. I see them. I recognize the posture, the hypervigilance, the way they learn to read rooms instead of trusting them. I don't need to know their names to feel connected to their experience.

Family, for me, is shared understanding. It is recognition without explanation. I see this redefinition reflected in my own children.

They talk about friends they consider family. People who feel like home, even if they don't share DNA. They move through the world with a fluid understanding of belonging, unconfined by rigid definitions. Watching that has been healing in ways I didn't expect.

It reminds me that family is not something you inherit. It is something you practice. **What does family mean to me now?**

It means *loving people* without **possession**.
It means *showing up* without **entitlement**.
It means *choosing connection* without **forcing permanence**.

I don't expect *handouts*.
I don't wait for someone to *rescue me*.
I don't confuse family with *obligation*.

I simply love people.

I try to be the safest version of myself I can be. I offer consistency where I can. I hold space without demanding loyalty. I listen more than I speak. I stay curious. I stay open.

I have learned that family is not about who claims you.

It is about who *respects* you.
It is not about who *names* you.
It is about who *sees* you.

Family is who allows you to arrive as you are and who does not punish you for needing time to trust. And maybe that is the truest definition I have:

Family is not the people you are told to belong to.

Family is the people who make belonging possible and safe, without condition.

Chapter Twenty-Eight

"You can tell the truth without carrying it everywhere."

I never wanted self-pity.

I never wanted anyone to feel sorry for me.

I learned early that sympathy can be another kind of distance. That being seen as fragile or broken can be just as isolating as being unseen at all. For a long time, I told my story to strangers with an openness that surprised even me. I could lay it all out without shaking, without pausing, without feeling much of anything. It was easier to speak when there was no expectation of relationship afterward.

But that version of me was still surviving.

I would be lying if I said it doesn't still hurt sometimes. There are days when the pain returns without warning… not sharp, not consuming, but present. A quiet ache that reminds me of what happened, of what was taken, of how much had to be endured before there was any space to rest.

The difference now is that I don't need to carry that pain into every room.

I don't owe my full story to everyone I meet. I don't need to spill my past to prove my strength or explain my boundaries. Healing taught me discernment. The ability to choose when and how my story is shared, and with whom. I speak now from a steadier place. From a version of myself who knows that truth does not require constant disclosure.

I am a *mother*.
I am someone who loves people without condition.
I am someone who had to learn that carrying
everything alone was not *strength*, it was **habit**.

There was a time when my story felt like a bag I dragged behind me everywhere I went. Heavy. Overfilled. Necessary for survival, but exhausting to carry. Therapy helped me understand that I could set it down without denying what it held.

One psychiatrist said something to me years ago that changed everything: You can't put time on healing.

That sentence felt revolutionary.

I had spent so long believing I should be *"over it"* by now. That there was some invisible deadline I had missed. That if I was still hurting, I must be doing something wrong. But healing isn't a task you complete. It's a relationship you build with yourself over time.

I was fortunate to work with a therapist for years. Someone who helped me learn how to be kind to myself. We spent sessions untangling the belief that mistakes were dangerous. That imperfection deserved punishment. That rest had to be earned.

I learned that *a mistake* does not result in being beaten.
That *discomfort* does not mean I've failed.
That I don't have to punish myself for not being perfect.

That grace applies to me, too. I am **not** damaged. I am **not** what happened to me.

It is not my role to be God, the judge, or the jury of my own life. I cannot explain why I went through what I did. I cannot explain why God allowed certain things to happen. I no longer waste energy trying to force meaning where answers do not exist.

What I can say is this: I have a **voice**. *We all do.*

We can use our stories to come together and help one another, or we can use our pain to keep hurting each other. I choose kindness. Not because I am naïve, but because I know how rare it is. I know what the absence of it does.

I love who I am now.

Not because I am healed completely, but because I am healing honestly.

And I don't need anyone else to validate that anymore.

Letter to Self *Journal Entry*

You are not that bag.

You are not the clothes shoved into it, the toys that didn't make the cut, the paperwork folded too many times. You are not the number written on a file, the placement you're sent to, or the labels people use because they don't know what else to call you.

That bag is not your identity.

It is evidence of a system that did not know how to hold you.

I know what it feels like to carry everything you own in something disposable. To be told, without words, that your life is temporary. I know how easy it is to believe that if your belongings can be thrown away, maybe you can be too.

Please hear this: you are not disposable.

You are learning how to survive in environments that would overwhelm most adults. You are adapting because you have to, not because you are broken. The skills you are developing now, awareness, resilience, intuition, are not flaws. One day, in the right spaces, they will become strengths.

If no one has told you this yet, let me be the one:

You deserved consistency.
You deserved honesty.
You deserved adults who showed up and stayed

If you are angry, you are not ungrateful.
If you are tired, you are not lazy.
If you are quiet, it does not mean you have nothing to say.

You are more than what you carry.

PART 6

WHAT REMAINS

Chapter Twenty-Nine

"We don't heal by becoming stronger. We heal by being met."

For most of my life, survival was the goal.

Not *healing*.
Not *happiness*.
Not *peace*.
Just **survival**.

There was a time when getting through the day felt like an accomplishment. When stability meant nothing catastrophic happened. When safety was defined not by comfort, but by the absence of immediate harm. I learned to live inside that narrow definition early, and I stayed there for a long time without questioning it.

Survival was **practical**.
Survival was **measurable**.
Survival was **praised**.

People told me I was strong. Resilient. Impressive. They pointed to what I had endured and spoke as if endurance itself was proof of healing. As if making it through meant I was fine. As if pain loses its impact just because you outlast it.

I accepted that narrative for years.

It gave people language they were comfortable admiring from a distance. It allowed them to feel inspired without having to sit with discomfort. It framed my life as a success story without asking what the cost had been.

But survival has a **limit**. And no one tells you what happens when you reach it.

The problem with survival is that it doesn't teach you how to live once the danger passes. It teaches you how to stay alert, how to brace, how to function under pressure, but it does not teach you how to soften. It does not teach you how to receive care. It does not teach you how to trust that something good will stay.

For a long time, I didn't realize that was what I was missing.
I thought something was wrong with me.

I thought maybe I was ungrateful. Or overly sensitive. Or incapable of enjoying the life I had built. I had done everything I was supposed to do. I had worked. I had stayed out of trouble. I had built a family. I had survived.

So *why* did calm feel so unfamiliar?
Why did rest feel undeserved?
Why did connection feel risky even when nothing
bad was happening?

Those questions didn't arrive all at once. They surfaced slowly, usually in moments when survival no longer had anything to respond to.

Quiet moments. Moments when nothing was wrong… yet my body stayed tense, my mind vigilant, my heart guarded.

That's when I began to understand something crucial: Survival had become my default setting. And it was no longer enough.

I had spent years adapting to instability, and that adaptation followed me into places where it no longer belonged. I knew how to read danger in a room faster than I knew how to relax in it. I knew how to anticipate disappointment before it happened. I knew how to leave emotionally before anyone else had the chance to leave me.

Those instincts once protected me. Now, they were isolating me.

There is a point in healing that doesn't look dramatic from the outside. No breakdown. No collapse. Just the quiet realization that the strategies you relied on no longer fit the life you're trying to live.

For me, that realization showed up in relationships.

I noticed how often I minimized my needs. How quickly I dismissed discomfort. How instinctively I took responsibility for other people's emotions. I noticed how hard it was to ask for help—and how easily I convinced myself I didn't need it.

I had learned early that needing less made me safer. But safety built on self-erasure is not safety. It's **containment**.

I had built a life where I was competent, reliable, and composed, but not fully present. I showed up, but I didn't always let myself be seen. I stayed useful, because usefulness felt like the closest thing to belonging I knew.

And *usefulness* is often rewarded. **Visibility** is not.

Healing, I learned, does not make you more palatable. It makes you more honest. And honesty invites critique.

As I began to speak more openly, *about my needs, my boundaries, my truth,* I noticed something unsettling: not everyone celebrated it. Some people grew uncomfortable. Some questioned my tone. Some preferred the quieter version of me, who adapted easily and asked for little.

There were critics. Not loud ones. Subtle ones.

The kind who framed discomfort as *concern*.
Who called boundaries *"distance."*
Who labeled clarity as *bitterness*.
Who preferred my survival to my *voice*.

For someone shaped by abandonment, that pushback was terrifying.

Survival had taught me that visibility comes with consequences. That being seen means being evaluated. That speaking too clearly can cost you connection.

Healing asked me to do it anyway. Being bold, I learned, is not about *confidence*. It's about **refusal**.

Refusal to **shrink** back into silence to preserve comfort.
Refusal to **explain** yourself into acceptability.
Refusal to **carry** other people's discomfort at the expense of your truth.

It is choosing to stand in your honesty even when criticism tries to pull you back into the safety of invisibility. Boldness came when I stopped negotiating my worth.

That didn't mean I stopped caring. It meant I stopped contorting.

I had to learn that not everyone will understand the version of you that no longer survives quietly, and that this is not a failure. It is evidence that you have changed.

Criticism, I realized, often arrives when you stop performing resilience and start practicing self-respect. And that criticism does not mean you are wrong. It means you are no longer invisible.

Healing did not begin when I became stronger. It began when I was met.

Met with **presence** instead of *pressure*.
Met with **curiosity** instead of *judgment*.
Met with **connection** that didn't require
performance.

Those moments taught my body what my mind already knew: safety is not an idea… it is a felt experience.

I began to understand that healing is not about becoming unbreakable. It is about becoming **reachable**.

Reachable to others.
Reachable to myself.

There are still days when survival whispers. When fear suggests I pull away. When old instincts tell me to stay quiet, stay agreeable, stay small. But now, I notice. And noticing gives me **choice**.

Choice to speak even when my voice shakes.
Choice to stay present when disappearing would feel
safer.
Choice to be bold, not because I am fearless, but
because I am done living half-visible.

Survival kept me alive. Connection is what allowed me to live. And courage, *the quiet, grounded kind,* is what keeps me here, choosing truth even when it costs me approval.

That is what remains.

Chapter Thirty

"What we needed was never perfection. It was genuine, nonjudgmental presence."

For a long time, I believed healing had a finish line. Not because anyone explicitly told me that, but because everything around me suggested it. Programs ended. Services closed. Eligibility expired. Timelines were marked by age, compliance, or progress measured on paper. There was always an implied *after*. A moment when support would no longer be necessary, when resilience would have done its job, when the story would shift from recovery to resolution.

But healing doesn't follow systems. And it doesn't end when the paperwork does.

What I understand now is that the question was never whether help existed. Often, it did. The deeper question was whether presence lasted long enough to matter.

I don't discount the role of programs. I wouldn't be honest if I did. Systems kept me alive when circumstances were unstable. Structure mattered. Routine mattered. Accountability mattered. There were moments when temporary support was the only thing standing between me and complete collapse.

But systems, by design, are finite. Human development is not.

Healing, *especially after prolonged trauma,* is not something you complete and set down. It is something you learn to carry with skill, patience, and support over time. It changes shape as you age. It resurfaces in new seasons. It asks new questions when life expands… through relationships, through parenting, through loss, through joy.

That doesn't mean systems fail. It means presence must outlast intervention.

For many years, I thought the goal was to become someone who no longer needed anything. Someone self-contained. Someone **"fully healed."** I chased that version of myself because it felt safer. Independence had always been rewarded. Need had always felt risky.

But that goal quietly harmed me.

It taught me to treat healing as a weakness to overcome instead of a process to respect. It taught me to hide ongoing struggles because I believed they signaled failure. It taught me that needing support past a certain point meant I wasn't doing something right.

None of that was true.

What *was* true was this: trauma does not disappear just because life becomes stable. It recalibrates. It shows up differently. It asks to be met again and again... sometimes gently, sometimes urgently.

And it asks for witnesses. I didn't need people to *save me*. I needed people **to stay**. That distinction took me years to understand.

As a teenager, I served on the Youth Advisory Board. At the time, I believed it was an opportunity, a chance to show adults that I wasn't what they expected. That I wasn't damaged, dangerous, or destined to fail. I wanted them to see that I was articulate, capable, responsible. That I could sit at tables meant for decision-makers and speak without falling apart.

I wanted to be evidence.

Looking back, I see something I couldn't see then. I wasn't just participating. I was performing safety.

I learned early that the quickest way to be spared further harm was to demonstrate usefulness. To show that I could contribute instead of collapse. The Youth Advisory Board gave me a sanctioned space to say, *Look at me. I'm not a problem. I'm helping.*

And I meant it.

I cared deeply. I listened carefully. I showed up prepared. I spoke when spoken to. I said the right things in the right tone. I learned the language adults trusted… policy, outcomes, improvement. I wanted to prove that children like me weren't just stories of failure.

What I didn't realize was how much pressure I was carrying inside my body.

Even in spaces meant for empowerment, I felt watched. Measured. Assessed. I understood, instinctively, that my presence represented more than just me. I was standing in for every foster kid who had ever been dismissed, every child who had been labeled difficult or ungrateful or too much.

I couldn't afford to be messy. So I wasn't.

I didn't speak about **fear**.
I didn't speak about **panic**.

I didn't speak about how my chest tightened before every meeting, how my mind raced long after the rooms emptied.

I spoke about solutions. I didn't yet understand that advocacy without safety becomes another form of survival.

What I see now is that I was still trying to prove I wasn't broken. Still trying to earn the right to exist without causing concern. Even while serving, even while helping shape conversations about youth voice, I hadn't learned how to inhabit my own.

I was visible, but not vulnerable. Present, but not at rest. The cost of that showed up later, in ways I didn't connect at the time.

Anxiety

Night arrives quietly,
but my body does not believe it.
My chest tightens first,
a pulse without rhythm,
a warning without language.

MILDRED ETHERTON

My heart stays in motion,
bracing for what will close next.
Thoughts splinter before I can stop them.

I try to step away from the fear,
but it folds me back into myself
breath repeating, panic swelling,
the quiet knowing
that another door is about to shut.

I breathe the way I was taught to.
In.
Out.
Slow enough to convince myself I am safe.

For a moment, it works.

Then the air thins.
My lungs forget how to trust.
My heart races as if it remembers
something my mind refuses to name.

I sing.
I walk.

THE LIE THAT NAMED ME

I read.
I do the things people suggest
when they mean well.

Music carries me briefly.
Nature softens the edges for a while.
Tasks distract. Pages turn.

But nighttime brings everything back,
the quiet magnifying what daylight lets me manage.

My throat tightens,
a locked gate holding words that never learned how to
leave.
The dark whispers familiar stories,
stay alert, stay ready, don't rest yet.

My body braces
for something unnamed,
as if fear itself is waiting
for permission to arrive.

This is not weakness.
This is a nervous system trained by vigilance.

A body shaped by environments
where stillness was never safe.

So I remind myself, gently:
I am here.
I am breathing.
This moment will not destroy me.

Calm comes.
Calm goes.
And I no longer punish myself for its absence.

Anxiety lived beneath my accomplishments for years,
tucked under professionalism and composure.
I learned how to be impressive
while unraveling quietly.

Now, I name it.
Not as failure.
Not as flaw.
But as evidence of survival,
and a body slowly learning
that the doors closing behind me
do not mean the world is ending.

Anxiety wasn't something I understood back then. It lived beneath my accomplishments, tucked under professionalism and composure. I learned how to be impressive while unraveling quietly.

Serving on the board gave me a seat at the table, but it didn't teach me how to rest in my own skin. That came later.

What I understand now is that my desire to serve was real, but it was also layered with something else: a need to prove that I wasn't dangerous, broken, or destined to fail. I wanted adults to see me as safe.

I didn't yet know that I was allowed to be human.

Advocacy without *safety* is **exhausting**.
Visibility without *support* is **destabilizing**.
Service without *self-compassion* eventually **collapses inward**.

None of this negates the value of youth voice. It complicates it.

Young people in systems are often given microphones before they are given stability. We are praised for speaking clearly while still bleeding quietly. We are celebrated for resilience without being offered rest.

If I could speak to that version of myself now, I would say this:

You didn't need to **prove** anything.
You were already *enough*.
Your worth was never dependent on how well you
represented survival.

The impact I could have had didn't require perfection. It required presence, not just for others, but for myself.

That understanding took years.

There were moments throughout my life when someone showed up briefly, long enough to interrupt isolation, long enough to remind me I wasn't invisible. Those moments mattered more than I could articulate at the time. They didn't erase what I had been through. They didn't undo damage. But they offered something survival alone never could: connection without condition.

Those moments didn't always come from people assigned to help me. Sometimes they came from educators who noticed effort instead of compliance. Sometimes from mentors who didn't need a title to invest. Sometimes from people who simply didn't disappear when things got complicated.

Presence does not require *perfection*. It requires **consistency**.

What I've learned, *slowly, unevenly,* is that consistency does something powerful to a nervous system shaped by instability. It teaches the body that safety doesn't always vanish. That care doesn't always come with a deadline. That connection doesn't have to be earned through performance.

That lesson doesn't arrive all at once. It arrives through repetition.

Through someone remembering your name.
Through someone asking how you're really doing,
and waiting for the answer.
Through someone staying when you don't have the
words yet.

I carry those moments with me now, not as proof that everything turned out fine, but as evidence that human connection leaves marks just as lasting as harm does.

For a long time, I thought my story was about survival. I see now that survival was only the beginning.

The deeper work, the work that continues, is learning how to live without bracing. Learning how to allow joy without immediately scanning for loss. Learning how to trust that support doesn't automatically come with an expiration date.

That work doesn't happen in *isolation*. It happens in **relationship**.

This is where hope lives, not in the absence of struggle, but in the presence of people who are willing to walk alongside it. Not in flawless systems, but in systems that understand their role as bridges, not destinations. Not in quick fixes, but in long-term commitment to human dignity.

I don't believe the answer is *fewer programs*. I believe the answer is **deeper continuity**.

Support that understands development doesn't move on a schedule. Care that adapts as people age instead of disappearing when they cross an arbitrary threshold. Communities that remain accessible when life looks *"stable"* on the outside but is still reorganizing on the inside.

This is a lifelong process. Not because people are broken, but because growth continues as long as life does.

I no longer measure healing by how little I need. I measure it by how honestly I can live.

By whether I can *ask for support* without shame.

By whether I can *stay connected* when fear tells me to withdraw.
By whether I can *extend to myself* the same grace I once believed was reserved for others.

What remains now is not the pain itself, but the **awareness** it created.

Awareness of how deeply connection shapes us.
Awareness of how absence leaves imprints.
Awareness that healing is not about becoming someone new.

It is about reclaiming the parts of yourself that adapted to survive and teaching them they no longer have to do that alone.

Hope, for me, is not **loud**. It is *steady*.

It lives in the belief that presence matters even when it's imperfect. That showing up counts even when you don't know what to say. That listening can be as transformative as intervention. And that the work does not end when services do.

This is not a story about overcoming everything. It is a story about continuing.

About *choosing connection* again and again.
About *staying engaged* with life even when it feels vulnerable.
About *trusting* that being seen, ***truly seen,*** is not something you age out of needing.

What remains is not just what survived. What remains is what continues to grow.

Chapter Thirty-Two
What Remains

"What we needed was never perfection. It was genuine, nonjudgmental presence."

This book is not about resilience.

It is about what happens when human connection is missing, and how powerful it is when it finally appears.

For a long time, I believed survival was the point. If I could just make it through the next day, the next move, the next version of myself, something would eventually settle. If I could only stop living in my head and make it stop thinking about every little thing. I mistook endurance for healing. I mistook spinning thoughts as truth. I learned to stay upright, to stay quiet, to stay useful. I believed silence was strength.

Survival kept me alive. **Connection** is what made me human again.

I learned early how to exist without expecting to be held. I learned how to read rooms quickly, how to adapt without asking, how to disappear just enough to avoid conflict. Belonging felt conditional. Safety felt revocable. Truth felt like something to manage carefully, not something to offer freely. I became skilled at making myself palatable.

I didn't ask for much. I didn't expect consistency. I learned how to accept fragments of care and call them enough. I learned how to move forward without anchoring myself to anyone or anywhere, because anchoring had always led to loss. That way of living worked… for a while.

But it came at a cost I didn't recognize until much later. It flattened my needs. It dulled my instincts. It taught me to measure my worth by how little space I took up in other people's lives. I confused independence with isolation. I confused resilience with numbness. I confused being unseen with being safe.

What no one told me was that the absence of connection doesn't just leave a gap. It reshapes you. It teaches you to doubt yourself. To question your perceptions. To believe that if something hurts, it must be because you're too sensitive or asking for too much. It teaches you to apologize for wanting what every human needs.

It took years for me to name that ache for what it was. *Not weakness. Not failure.* A hunger for **basic human connection**.

The kind that doesn't require performance.
The kind that doesn't disappear when you make a mistake.
The kind that **stays**.

I didn't find that connection all at once. I found it in pieces, in moments that didn't look dramatic from the outside. A teacher who noticed effort. A social worker who remembered my name. A staff member who spoke to me like I mattered. A friend who stayed even when I didn't know how to explain myself. None of these moments fixed everything. But they interrupted the silence just enough to remind me I existed.

And later, in my children.

They didn't heal my past. But they revealed it. They showed me how deeply connection shapes us, how much damage is done when it's missing, and how powerful it is when it's offered freely. Loving them forced me to confront what I had normalized. It forced me to see how often I had been told to be grateful for survival instead of being supported in healing.

That realization reframed everything. We do not suffer because we are **broken**. We suffer because we were not met.

Children are not resilient by nature. They become resilient because they have no other choice. What we call strength is often adaptation. What we praise as independence is often abandonment in disguise. I lived most of my life adapting… anticipating danger before it arrived, softening my voice, carrying responsibility that was never mine, protecting others at the expense of myself. Those skills kept me alive. They also kept me distant.

Healing, for me, did not look like forgetting. It looked like allowing myself to be seen without armor. It looked like learning that connection doesn't have to be earned through usefulness or compliance. It looked like staying present even when fear told me to retreat.

That learning was slow. Uneven. Uncomfortable.

There were times I wanted to retreat back into survival mode because it felt familiar... predictable, safer than vulnerability. But familiarity is not the same as safety, and I had spent too many years confusing the two. I had to relearn what it meant to **belong**.

Belonging is not being tolerated. It is being **welcomed**.
Belonging is not being needed. It is being **chosen**.
Belonging is not silence. It is being **heard** without punishment.

These truths sound simple. They are not. They require systems to change. They require adults to stay. They require listening when it would be easier to look away. They require us to believe that connection is not a luxury—it is a necessity.

I often think about the children who are still learning how to carry their lives in pieces. About the adults they will become if we continue to prioritize efficiency over humanity. About the stories that will go untold because no one slowed down long enough to listen. We do not need more programs that teach children how to survive. We need relationships that show them they are worth staying for.

What we miss most, though, is the power of staying when nothing is wrong.

Connection is often framed as intervention… showing up when a child is in crisis, when behavior escalates, when something breaks. But the moments that mattered most in my life were quieter than that. They were the check-ins that came without urgency. The adults who showed up when there was nothing to fix. The consistency that said, *I see you even when you're okay.*

So much of my life was shaped by people appearing only when something went wrong, and disappearing again once the immediate concern passed. That pattern taught me to associate attention with danger, care with consequence. It taught me to brace when someone noticed me, to expect that connection would be brief and conditional.

What I needed, what so many of us needed, was someone who stayed present in the in-between. Someone who checked in without suspicion. Someone who showed up not because there was a problem, but because there was a relationship.

Consistency builds safety in ways crisis response never can.

When someone checks in regularly, without agenda, without documentation, without an outcome to report, it teaches the nervous system something new. It teaches that connection doesn't always precede loss. That attention doesn't always signal punishment. That care can exist without strings attached.

Staying matters more than saving.

You don't have to have the right words. You don't have to fix anything. You don't have to wait until something is broken to reach out. A text. A call. A remembered birthday. A *"thinking of you."* A steady presence that doesn't disappear once things look stable.

Because stability is fragile when it's never been modeled.

And healing does not happen only in moments of collapse. It happens in the quiet accumulation of being remembered. Being expected. Being noticed even when you are not asking to be.

If there is one thing I wish more people understood, it is this: consistency is not small. Staying is not passive. Checking in when everything seems fine can be the very thing that keeps it that way.

For children, and adults, who grew up without permanence, showing up without crisis is just as important.

This is not a rejection of help or structure. Programs matter. Policies matter. Support matters. But none of it works without presence. None of it heals without continuity. Temporary solutions cannot meet lifelong wounds. People do not outgrow the need to be seen.

If this book has taught me anything, it is this: what we remember most is not what happened to us, but who was there when it did. *Who noticed. Who stayed. Who didn't make us carry it alone.*

I survived many things. What changed me was connection.

Not the *perfect kind*.
Not the kind that *fixes everything*.
The kind that **shows up anyway**.

If you are reading this as someone who works inside a system, I hope you remember that your presence matters more than your policies. If you are reading this as a teacher, I hope you know that noticing one child can alter the course of a life. If you are reading this as a parent, I hope you understand that repair is more powerful than perfection.

And if you are reading this as someone who has always felt different, out of place, or unseen, I want you to hear this clearly:

There was nothing wrong with you.

You adapted because you had to. You survived because no one showed you another way. The parts of you that learned to stay quiet, to stay small, to stay alert... they are not flaws. They are evidence of intelligence in the absence of safety.

But you are allowed to want more than survival.

You are allowed to want connection that does not cost you your voice. You are allowed to build a life where honesty is not punished, and presence is not temporary. You are allowed to be held.

This is what remains when everything else falls away:

The need to be *seen*.
The need to be *heard*.
The need to *belong*.
Not *someday*.
Not *conditionally*.
Now.

If you are listening and showing up... *please, don't stop*.

Chapter Thirty-Three
Called to Love

"Some people are born into comfort.
Some are born into chaos.
Some are born into stories they never chose.
But somewhere along the way, every one of us must
decide what kind of heart we will carry through the
world."

If I am honest, my life has been far from fair. But what does *fair* even mean?

Who gets to decide that?

Before I ever took my first breath, my life was already tangled in a secret I did not create. I was born into a complicated love triangle, a truth hidden long before I was old enough to understand it. My mother's husband knew I was not his child, and that resentment quietly lived inside our home.

Three adults, my mother, my biological father, and the man who raised me, believed they would take that secret with them to their graves.

In many ways, they almost did.

Both of my parents were already gone, already in heaven, before I learned the truth about who I really was. Before I could ask questions. Before I could understand what it meant.

For years, I carried a name and a story that were built on silence.

When the truth finally surfaced, it hurt more than I can fully explain. But it also gave me something unexpected.

Freedom.

Freedom to stop living inside a lie. Freedom to stop pretending that a story belonged to me when it never truly did. By the time I learned the truth, I had already lost so much.

I *lost* my siblings when we were taken from our home.
I *lost* the family unit we once had.
I *lost* the illusion of safety that every child deserves.

Then I was returned to the same environment and endured years of abuse. For most of my life, I carried the quiet belief that I did not truly belong anywhere.

I *watched* other children get adopted.
I *watched* families stay together.
I *watched* people inherit homes, stability, and
opportunities that seemed to appear effortlessly.

Sometimes I even watched people who never seemed to work for anything at all, yet somehow always had everything handed to them.

Homes.
Cars.
Security.
Support.

Meanwhile, I was fighting just to **survive**.

Trying to keep food on the table.
Trying to stay afloat.
Trying to build a life with my own hands.

My husband owns a construction business, and over the years, I have watched something that has always bothered me deeply.

People will hire him.
They will praise his work.
They will thank him when the job is finished.

And then when it comes time to pay, something changes.

Suddenly, there are complaints.
Suddenly, there are excuses.
Suddenly, people decide the work was not worth
what they originally agreed to.

What I have realized is that sometimes people decide another person's worth based on what *they think that person deserves*. They measure someone else's labor, time, and effort through their own lens.

And that hurts. Not just *financially*. But **personally**.

Because when you spend enough years watching these things happen, it becomes very easy to start comparing your life to everyone else's.

Comparison is a quiet thief. It creeps into your thoughts and starts whispering things like:

Why does their life look easier?
Why do they get the opportunities?
Why do they have the family, the house, the stability?

I had to learn something the hard way. Comparing our lives will slowly poison our hearts. Because the truth is that every person carries battles we cannot see. And every life holds pain that is hidden behind closed doors.

Even in my own home, I hear it sometimes from my children. *"That's not fair."*

And they are right. Life is not always fair.

But I have also learned something else. Fairness was never promised. There have been moments in my life when bitterness tried to take root inside me.

Moments when I felt angry at the world. Moments when I wanted to give up completely. Pain does strange things to people.

Sometimes it makes us push others away before they can hurt us.
Sometimes it makes us build walls so thick that no one can get close.
And *sometimes* pain makes us hurt people who never deserved it.

I wish I could say that I have always handled my pain perfectly. But that would not be the truth. There were times when I said cruel things. There were times when I pushed people away.

And there were even times when I made up things about people that were not true simply because I wanted them to hurt the way I was hurting.

That is not something I am proud of. But it is something I am honest about. Because healing requires truth.

Wounded people sometimes wound others. And becoming a different version of myself took years of reflection, humility, prayer, and growth. But one thing has always remained true. My story may have started with brokenness, but brokenness did not get to decide who I would become.

Yes, there are still things I dream about.

I *want* a home that truly belongs to my family.
I *want* a vehicle big enough for all of us.
I *want* to take vacations without worrying about
every dollar.
I *want* to stop living paycheck to paycheck.
I *want* to help my children go to college if that is the
path they choose.
I *want* to buy them their first car.
I *want* to know that if something ever happened to
my husband or me, they would be okay.

But some of the things I want most in this life are things
money could never buy.

I **wish** my parents could sit at my kitchen table once
a week for dinner.
I **wish** all my siblings and their children could
gather together in one room, laughing and sharing
stories.
I **wish** my children could know their grandparents
on my side of the family.

Those are the kinds of things this world can never give
back. And yet, even with all that loss, I have learned
something beautiful. My favorite moments in life are the
simple ones.

Cooking dinner. Calling my family to the table. Watching my husband and children sit together and talk about their day.

Those moments feel like small pieces of heaven to me. Somewhere along the way, I realized that bitterness would only steal more of my life.

So I made a *choice*. I chose **gratitude**. Not because life suddenly became easy. But because gratitude reminds me that God is still present even in the hard chapters.

Scripture says:

> *"He has shown you, O man, what is good;*
> *and what does the Lord require of you*
> *but to act justly, love mercy,*
> *and walk humbly with your God."*
> — Micah 6:8

God never promised life would be fair. Even Jesus faced betrayal, cruelty, and suffering. But He still chose love. And that is the example I try to follow.

Every person will experience *injustice*. Every person will feel ***pain***.

The real question is not whether life will be *unfair*. The real question is what we will do with the unfairness.

Will we let it make us bitter? Or will we let it make us compassionate?

When my life is over, my legacy will not be measured in money or possessions. None of those things follow us into eternity. **But love does.**

My greatest hope is that my children grow into people who are kind.

People who *forgive*.
People who *show mercy*.
People who *love others* the way God has loved us.

Because in the end, I believe God will care far less about how perfect we were and far more about how we treated one another.

Did we love?
Did we forgive?
Did we extend grace when it was hard?

Life may not always be fair. But every single day, we are given something better than fairness.

We are given *mercy*.
We are given *grace*.
And we are given *another chance* to love someone.

So if you are reading this, let this be my message to you.

Call someone you love.

Apologize if you need to.

Forgive someone who hurt you.

Check on people even when they seem fine.

Spread kindness wherever you go.

Because love will always outlive pain.

And that is why I am still here.

A lie may have named me.

But love is what defined me.

And love is what I chose anyway.

A Letter to the Reader — My Testimony

If you've made it to the end of this book, then you've already seen it.

Not the polished version. Not the version people are comfortable telling.

You've seen the broken pieces. The silence. The things most people spend their entire lives trying to hide.

For a long time, I believed my story was supposed to stay hidden, too.

Because silence felt safer. Safer than telling the truth.

Safer than letting anyone see how much my childhood actually broke me... and how long I carried that into my adult life.

But silence doesn't protect you. It traps you.

It keeps shame alive. It convinces you that you are the only one who has ever felt this alone.

And loneliness has followed me for most of my life.

Even in rooms full of people.

Even inside families.
Even inside places that were supposed to feel safe.

I often felt like I was just outside of my own life...
watching everyone else belong somewhere... While I was
still trying to figure out who I was supposed to be.

I was forced to go to church as a child.

Every week we sat in those pews.
We listened to sermons about love.
About forgiveness.
About God.

And then we went home... to abuse.

As a child, that kind of contradiction confuses your soul.

You sit there wondering:

If God is love... why does this still happen?

If church is supposed to be safe... why does no one see
what is happening behind closed doors?

And I think that is something we still struggle with today.

We have become very comfortable judging each other.

Judging people by their past.
Judging people by their mistakes.
Judging people by the families they came from.
Judging people by how broken their stories look from the outside.

But the truth is, none of us arrived here perfect.

Not one of us.

Some people simply had safer places to grow.
Some people had parents who protected them.
Some people had stability that others never experienced.

But that doesn't make anyone more worthy of love.

And yet sometimes the places that talk the most about love, can also become the places where people feel the most judged.

Where we smile on Sunday... but ignore suffering the rest of the week.

Where we talk about grace... but struggle to give it.

Where we praise God with our voices... but forget to love the people standing right next to us.

That is not the love Christ showed.

Christ never asked where someone came from before loving them.

He never asked how clean their past was
He never asked if their life looked respectable enough.
He simply loved them.

And if we are going to call ourselves followers of Christ, then we must start loving people the same way.

Not perfect love.
Messy love.
Not easy love.
But love lived with intention.
Love lived with connection.

When I was thirteen years old, I was baptized.

I remember standing there in that church with a broken arm.

A child carrying wounds people could see... and wounds they couldn't.

And sitting in that same church was the man who abused me.

Watching.

Sometimes I wonder if he believed that somehow made things better.

Maybe he thought that if I had God, someday I would forgive him.

But forgiveness is not pretending something never happened.

Forgiveness is refusing to let evil have the final word in your life.

And what still sits heavy in my heart is this:

That same year, I was baptized... was the same year I was taken away from my siblings again.

This time for good.

That was the year we were separated forever.

The year I stood in church being told I belonged to the family of God… was the same year I lost the only family I had left.

That kind of loss changes a person.

And for a long time… it changed me in ways I didn't understand.

I learned how to survive.

I learned how to rely on myself. How to carry things I was never meant to carry.

And from the outside, that probably looked like strength.

But survival is heavy.

It's waking up already tired.

It's never feeling like you fully belong anywhere.

And for most of my life, that's how I lived.

Until there was a moment... where everything almost ended.

I was almost thirty years old.

I had two little girls.

Two girls who trusted me to be their safe place... when I had never truly experienced what that felt like myself.

And I remember sitting there thinking...

Maybe the world would be better without me in it.

Maybe the pain would finally stop.

There was no reason, based on my life, to believe things would get better.

No pattern of things working out.

No evidence that something would change.

And yet... something did.

Not around me. In me.

There wasn't a voice. There wasn't a moment I could point to and explain.

But there was a shift.

A quiet, steady thought that cut through everything else: You still have a choice.

And for the first time in my life, that choice didn't feel like pressure.

It felt like something holding me... when I didn't have the strength to hold myself together anymore.

Nothing about my past changed.

Nothing was erased.

But something in me did.

The weight didn't feel final anymore. The pain didn't feel like it had the last word.

And I realized something I had never understood before...
I may never have the answers.

I may never understand why certain things happened.

Why some children are loved and protected... and others are left to survive things they should never have to survive.

I don't have an explanation for that.

But I do know this.

Everything in my life should have turned me into someone who stopped loving.

Everything should have hardened me.
Closed me off.
Made me believe that people weren't worth it.

And it didn't.

Not because I'm strong. Not because I figured everything out. But because something met me in the middle of my lowest moment... when I had nothing left.

And I can't explain that without God. Not the version people sometimes show.

But a God who meets people in broken places. A God who doesn't wait for your life to look put together. A God who stays... even when everything else has left.

So if you're reading this and you don't believe — I understand that.

I did too. But I'm not asking you to believe because someone told you to.

I'm asking you to consider this... What if the very thing you think disqualifies you... is actually the place where you could be met?

What if your questions don't push God away... but bring you closer to something real?

What if your story isn't something to hide... but something that still has purpose?

Because I am living proof that even when you don't understand... even when nothing makes sense... even when your life does not look like it should... it is not over.

You are not too far gone.

You are not too broken.
And your life is not beyond meaning.

And I may never understand why my life started the way
it did.

But I do know this. Even the life that begins in silence can
become a voice that helps others find their way home.

Chapter Thirty-Four

*The Girl I Had to Become For Myself. "She wasn't hard to love… She was just never loved the way she needed."**

People say healing your inner child like it's simple. Like it's something soft. Something gentle. Something you do with a journal and a few kind words.

But for me… it didn't feel like that. It felt like **grief**.

The kind of grief you can't explain.
The kind that doesn't have a funeral.
The kind that just lives in you… quietly.

I remember being told to write a letter to my younger self by my therapist. To be kind to her. To give her what she never had.

I didn't understand it. I just knew I didn't want to feel like this anymore.

So I wrote the letter anyway. And nothing changed. At least… not right away.

Life kept moving.
I got older.
I became a **mother**.

And then one day, without warning, in the middle of something ordinary, it hit me.

Watching my children *laugh*.
Watching them *be held*.
Watching them *be seen*.

I realized something I had never fully let myself feel before. That little girl in me… was *never* held like that.

No one slowed down for her.
No one studied her.
No one made her feel like she was something to be cherished.

And suddenly, the letter I had written years before… meant something different. Because now I understood what she needed. And I understood… that no one was coming back to give it to her.

Except me… and the part I never expected?

When my life started to fall apart… when the truth of my life came crashing in… when I felt like I was unraveling, she didn't disappear.

That little girl didn't leave me. She showed up.

And this time… I didn't ignore her.

Journal Entry

Dear Little Millie,

I wish I could sit next to you. Not to fix anything. Not to tell you it all gets better.

Just to sit with you... so you don't have to feel so alone.

I think about the way you used to look around... always trying to understand what you did wrong.

Why things felt different for you.

Why love felt like something everyone else received so easily... but for you, it always felt just out of reach.

You carried that question everywhere. Why wasn't I wanted?

You didn't always say it. But it was there.

In the way you stayed quiet.

In the way you watched instead of spoke.

In the way you tried to be easy to love.

I know your birthdays didn't feel like they belonged to you.

I know what it felt like to wake up that day... hoping, just a little, that maybe this time would be different.

Maybe someone would notice.
Maybe someone would make you feel special.
Maybe someone would celebrate you.

But most of the time... it passed like any other day. And you learned not to expect anything. Because expecting something hurt more.

I know holidays were the same.

You didn't ask for much. Just small things. Things that mattered to you. But what you really wanted... you didn't know how to ask for.

You wanted someone to sit with you.
To look at you.
To care about what mattered to you.
You wanted connection.
You wanted to feel like you belonged somewhere. And instead... you felt like you were just there.

1 to be fixed, you were never daddy's little girl.

1 know you tried to make sense of things that never made sense.

And somehow... you still tried.

You tried to be good.

You tried to protect your siblings.

You tried to be someone worth loving.

You carried pain you didn't have words for.

And when no one came... you carried it alone.

So you started to believe something about yourself.

That maybe you were the reason.

That maybe you weren't enough.

That maybe if you were different... someone would stay.

But listen to me. You were never the reason. You were a child. A child who needed love. And didn't receive it. That is not your fault. There was always something in you.

Something steady. Something that refused to disappear... no matter how much you were overlooked.

You dreamed of a family. A real one. Not perfect. Just safe.

And you held onto that... even when you had no proof it could exist. And somehow... you built it.

Out of nothing.
Out of pain.
Out of everything you didn't have.

You became everything you needed. And I need you to hear this. Really hear it. I am proud of you.

Not for surviving. But for who you chose to be after everything you went through.

You didn't become cold.
You didn't become cruel.
You didn't become what hurt you.
You became love.

And I see you. I choose you. And I am not going anywhere.

Love,

Me

Journal Entry:

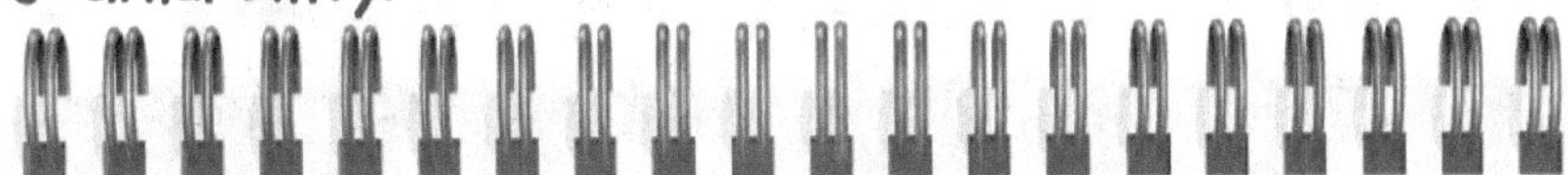

Dear Big Me,

I see you.

Even when you think you're hiding it... I still see you.

I see how tired you are. Not the kind of tired that sleep fixes.

The kind where your heart feels heavy... and you don't want to be strong anymore.

I see when people say they'll be there... and then they're not.

And I see how you try to act like it doesn't hurt. But it does.

I hear the things you tell yourself.

That maybe something is wrong with you.
That maybe you're too much.
That maybe the way you felt when you were me... was right.
But I don't believe that. I think you love really big.

And I think people don't always know what to do with that.

I know you're hurting about the truth.

About where you came from.

I know you thought that when you finally found out... something inside of you would finally feel different.

Like maybe it would fix that empty feeling.

Like maybe it would make everything make sense.

But it didn't. Because you weren't looking for a new story.

You were looking for closure. You just wanted to understand.

You just wanted to know where you came from... so you could understand who you are.

Not to erase your past. Not to pretend it didn't happen.

Just to make sense of it. And even when it didn't give you the peace you hoped for... you still faced it.

You didn't run. You didn't hide. You stood in the truth. And I'm really proud of you for that. I see you living in your truth now.

Even though your whole life felt like something you couldn't fully understand. That matters.

I know you still want a family. Not a perfect one.

Just one where you can sit together... and feel like you belong.

I know that's all you've ever wanted. But I need to tell you something.

If I had you as my mom... I would never wonder if I was loved.

Because I see you.

I see you try.
I see you keep going.
I see you love even when it's hard.

You're not broken. You're not damaged.

You're someone who went through things most people don't understand... and you still chose to be kind.

You don't have to keep proving anything. You already did enough.

You are allowed to rest. You are allowed to be loved. And you do belong. You always did. I'm really proud of you.

Love,
Little Me

And maybe healing isn't loud. Maybe it doesn't look like everything is suddenly making sense. Maybe it looks like this instead.

A quiet moment.

Where you finally stop running from the past… and sit beside it. Where you look at the version of you who went through it.

The **one** who waited. The **one** who wondered why she wasn't chosen. The **one** who learned how to survive before she ever learned how to feel safe, and you don't leave her there.

You *stay*.
You *sit* with her.
You ***tell her*** the truth she needed all along.

That she was always *worthy*.
That she was **never** the problem.
That she was **never** hard to love.
She was just… never loved the way she *needed*.

And maybe that's the moment everything shifts. Not because the past changes. But because she finally understands… she isn't waiting anymore.

Because the person she needed… finally came back for her.

And this time, ***she stayed.***

I stayed.

For the little girl who learned how to be strong
before she ever felt safe…
I came back for you.
And this time,
I stayed.

About the Author

Millie holds a Bachelor's degree in Human Services and has pursued education as both a tool for understanding trauma and a pathway toward meaningful change. She is a co-author of *Victorious Transformation* and aspires to advocate for youth in care by demonstrating that survival is not the finish line, and that people deserve time, support, and grace to understand who they are after it ends.

Having spent a decade as a ward of the state, her work is rooted not in theory, but in lived experience.

Married and the mother of four wonderful children, Millie is deeply committed to restoring basic human connection, believing that showing up, listening, and bearing witness can be as transformative as any formal intervention.

When she is not writing, Millie enjoys journaling, music, gardening, cooking, and spending time outdoors. Through her work and her words, she hopes to create space for understanding, dignity, and connection, especially for those who were never meant to face life alone.